The Joy of Financial Freedom

A Biblical and Practical Guide to Becoming Debt-Free

Gwynedd Jones

First Edition 2021

Streetlamp Publishers

streetlamppublishers@gmail.com

ISBN: 978-0-9934165-8-3

Cover: rhysllwyd.com

"Keep out of debt and owe no man anything, except to love one another….."

(Romans 13:8a - AMPC)

The practical steps relating to debt-freedom shared in this book are not meant to replace nor be a substitute for sound counsel offered by accredited debt-management organizations. These practical steps are drawn from our personal experience, and should therefore be viewed as additional tools to any counsel individuals may already be receiving.

Contents

Part 3 – God's Financial System

Part 4 – Practical Stewardship

Dedicated to my wife Jill, for her amazing faithfulness.

Jill – I see Jesus in you.

Introduction

The subject of money provokes different responses from different people within the Body of Christ (the Church). Some regard money as evil, while others see it as a blessing. Some see money as a tool for good; others see it as a taboo subject that is difficult to discuss. There are some who take a lifetime vow of poverty; and then others who believe in abundant prosperity. It's understandable therefore why the 'average' Christian is a bit confused about what the Bible says about money, considering there are so many different and often contradictory beliefs. This may be one reason why a lot of Christians are stuck somewhere in the middle – not knowing what the Bible *really* teaches about money. Some are not clear whether money is evil or not, while others have become accustomed to struggling financially each month, thinking it's God's will. Then there are others who do have money to spare, but they lack a freedom to spend it on themselves because they don't know what God's thoughts are on the matter.

This book has not been written to try to untangle all those various viewpoints, but rather is meant to bring clarity to one particular truth the Bible teaches about money. That truth is - *God wants His people to be financially debt-free*. Whatever your personal view of money is, I would ask you to lay it aside for a moment so you don't miss this one important truth from the Bible - *God wants His people to be financially debt-free*.

The debt of sin owed by mankind has already been paid on Calvary when God sent His Son Jesus to die for the sin of the world. By one lavish act of grace Jesus paid the greatest debt man owes so we could walk free. That grace brought *spiritual* freedom, but God's will is for people to also walk in a *practical* freedom. God wants people to be free to enjoy their *everyday* lives, which is why Jesus said He came to give *abundant* life, not a 'I'll be happy if I can scrape through' sort of life (John 10:10). Financial debt is not enjoyable, and because God loves us, He wants to bring us out of debt so we can enjoy a life of financial freedom. From God's perspective, clearing our debt of sin at Calvary is only the starting point to bringing His children into their full inheritance. Included in the Christian's salvation is the deliverance from the bondage financial debt brings so we can enjoy the life God intended us to have - to the full.

Though we may not actually be aware of it, financial debt brings a yoke that we carry with us everywhere. It dictates to us where we're able to go, and limits us in what we're able to do. That's because the one who borrows (the one who is in debt) is always subject to the one who lends (Proverbs 22:7). It's not in God's plan for anything nor anyone to have mastery over us because it's for *freedom* that Christ has set us free (Galatians 5:1). For any financial lender to have mastery over a child of God is therefore contrary to the Father's plan for their lives. The only One we should be subject to is God Himself, and we're given the freedom to make that choice by receiving Jesus as the Lord of our lives. When God calls us in a particular direction, no matter how passionate and willing we may be to follow His leading, financial debt will limit the calling because we're subject to the one who we're borrowing from. What debt freedom brings is a release from the yoke so we have a full and unrestricted liberty to follow the will of God for our lives. His will is to free us from the shackles of financial debt, allowing us to follow Him unhindered.

Introduction

As well as bringing clarity to the Biblical truth that God wants His people to be financially debt-free; this book is also written to help people in a *practical* way, which is why you will see the boxes titled 'Practical Exercise'. The exercises in the early part of the book are there to help grasp the *vision, as well as the faith* needed to move towards the goal of becoming debt-free. Then continuing through the book, the focus shifts more towards exercises that help the individual *become more organized* in their finances. Both are needed to see victory – a foundation of faith and vision, as well as an understanding of the practicalities of dealing with money on a day-to-day basis.

Some of the practical suggestions are relatively easy and quick to do; others will require more time and effort to get the full benefit from them. When faith in God for debt-freedom is birthed, the majority of us start to hope that somehow there's a 'quick-fix' solution – even hoping God will miraculously send all the money we need in one big lump sum so that we can clear our debt overnight. This was certainly true of me when I was looking to become debt-free! What my wife Jill and I experienced however was that debt-freedom is a journey, and as with any journey we needed to take one step at a time.

I would encourage the reader to view these practical exercises as small steps, each one taking them closer towards their goal of becoming debt-free. Ideally, each exercise should be completed before moving on to read the next chapter, because they are ordered in a particular way. Once the target of debt freedom is reached, these practical measures will also have helped equip the individual so that God can take them to the next level of their journey with Him. As we walk with Him, let's take Jesus' advice to *"Have faith in God"!* (Mark 11:22).

A Personal Testimony

Growing up as a child left me with a lot of insecurities. One symptom of this insecurity began to show itself in my mid-twenties when I became passionate about saving money. I was married to Jill by this time, and even though saving money is a good thing, my desire to 'save for a rainy day' became somewhat of an obsession. Looking at a growing bank account made me feel good, which I didn't realize at the time was the result of putting my security in money. Money was becoming my 'god'. The more money I had, the more secure I felt, because naively I thought money was the answer to every problem I might face. With the arrival of our two children, I was persuaded to put the money to good use – we extended the small bungalow we were living in so we could have more room as a family. Once it was spent however, I was driven to start saving again because I felt vulnerable looking at a depleted bank account.

Everything changed for me when I became a Christian at the age of thirty-one. In the process of giving my heart to the Lord, I understood my decision to make Him first in my life also meant I was letting go of money as my security – which I did. Once I'd made the commitment, I soon realized I had no idea what a healthy relationship with money looked like, because I didn't know in those early days what the Bible taught about money. Was I meant to give everything away? Was money evil? Unsurprisingly, a barrage of unanswered questions left me extremely confused. I was keen to get it right, so part of my journey in following Christ over the last 30 years or so has involved discovering what the Bible says about money.

In the early years of our marriage Jill and I had a very healthy income compared to the average household. Despite this, we carried a lot of debt and had no plan for getting rid of it. We thought debt was normal. Even though the debt made me feel uncomfortable, we had bigger issues to deal with, so getting rid of it wasn't a priority. The nature of debt is that it eats into the first part of an income every month, and that was certainly true for us. We would pay what we owed at the start of the month, but by the end of the month we'd find ourselves short despite our healthy income. This was a cycle that continually repeated itself. We weren't being extravagant – it was down to not understanding what the Bible taught about money, as well as not budgeting what we had in our possession. We'd never been taught how to budget, so we often bought things without actually knowing whether we could afford them or not.

I'd had a desire to study the Bible (in a formal way) for a few years after becoming a Christian, and at the turn of the millennium (2000) that opportunity finally presented itself. Jill and I agreed for me to go down to working part-time, and with this decision came a reduction in income of forty percent. We were happy to take this step of faith because we both knew it was the right thing to do as we followed Jesus. Despite this sizeable reduction, God performed one of the biggest miracles to date regarding our finances. We still weren't budgeting properly, and were still living from one month to the next as far as our income was concerned, but now on a reduced amount. Yet within 14 months the Lord brought us to a place where we were able to clear our mortgage. It didn't make sense to the natural mind, which is why we still regard it as a miracle.

Even after our mortgage was cleared, we still weren't completely debt-free because we were continually overdrawn in our bank account, only clearing the overdraft when our next salary came in. It was about three years later that we finally became fully debt-free. By God's grace we were taught how to put together an extremely simple budget plan that encouraged us to allocate money, and then to make sure we put boundaries on our spending.

Despite the financial challenges over the years, because of God's goodness we have remained debt-free. It's not always been easy and we've needed to take a stand of faith many times in what we know to be true from the Bible. Our experience however is that when we are willing to faithfully commit our finances to the Lord, He will take us on a journey which not only includes His faithful provision, but also includes a unique and tailored plan to help us become debt-free. Even those times when we find ourselves in lack as a result of our own poor choices, He will not abandon us but will help us learn lessons that equip us as we go forward.

We've shared our testimony in order to help the reader understand this book has not been written as a theory. It's written from a perspective born out of *experience* - the experience of putting our faith in what the Bible teaches about God's faithfulness and seeing Him bring us through. As you journey through the book on your way to debt freedom, we're with you on that journey. We're not alien to the experiences of what being in debt brings. We know what it means to have a deep desire to one day be free from owing money to people and institutions. We also know what it feels like when an unexpected bill comes in (no matter how small it may be), not knowing where the money to pay for it will come from.

Then there's the 'mind games' that the devil brings to try to convince us that God won't bring us through 'this time'. These challenges are real, and they're unpleasant, but we've experienced over the years that if we stand on God's promises, His faithfulness will bring us through to the other side. Despite all the challenges and hardships we've faced, both Jill and I are here to tell you that sticking with God is worth it! Continue to draw near to Him for your breakthrough, and He will draw near to you (James 4:8).

Part 1

Bringing Hope

1

Borrowing is Not Sinful

A person is regarded as being in financial debt when they owe money to someone. It could be as a result of taking a loan to buy a car, a mortgage to buy a house, having one or more credit cards, or even simply borrowing money from a friend which they haven't yet repaid. Unfortunately, many people view financial debt as a normal part of life. The constant advertising of credit cards, instant loans, and interest free credit further reinforces the image that borrowing money is normal, leaving people conditioned to think there is no other way to live other than to be in debt. As a result, some people's expectation to live a debt-free life remains low. Living with the constant burden of debt may be normal from a *worldly* perspective, but from a Biblical viewpoint it is *abnormal*. The Biblical perspective towards financial debt is *totally the opposite* to how the world views it.

The Bible does not condemn the individual who is in debt, but it does make it clear what the dangers are for those who *are* in debt. This is why having financial debt is not the normal way for a Christian to live. The first revelation we need to get regarding debt is that for followers of Christ, *debt shouldn't be regarded as normal*, so we shouldn't be tolerating it. God has planned a better way for His people to live regarding finances, which includes being totally free from the yoke that financial debt brings.

The Christian who has been born-again through faith in Christ no longer lives in the kingdom of the world[1] where debt is regarded as normal, but rather lives in the Kingdom of God where debt is *abnormal*. Because they've been transferred to a new kingdom through faith in Christ[2], they now live in a kingdom that has a different set of values, and a different set of norms to the one they escaped from. Many Christians fail to realize their faith in Christ has transferred them into this new kingdom, and so sadly remain stuck in the ways of the old one even though they've been rescued from it. They miss out on the benefits (the blessings) this new kingdom affords them, one of which is to be able to live without debt.

There may be aspects of these first two chapters that are challenging to the person who is in debt, because it touches on some of the strong things the Bible says about borrowing. As we'll see, the Bible does not condemn borrowing, but neither does it pull any punches when talking about it. The aim is not to make the individual feel condemned or guilty about financial debt – in fact it's the total opposite - it is meant to bring freedom.

Chapters one and two are written for the purpose of gently waking people up to the dangers debt can bring. They're meant to shake the reader out of any apathy they may be feeling towards debt, so they become stirred up and motivated to seek God's help on how to become free. Financial debt is a serious issue from God's perspective because He knows the misery and bondage it can bring. Once we see debt the way God sees it, we'll want to seek His help to get rid of it. The good news is that God is waiting for us to ask Him for His help. He has a plan for our lives that will release us from the slavery that financial debt brings. That's good news!

Borrowing is Not Sinful

God has set out some principles in the Bible for those who lend money to others[3], so lending is not sinful. If _lending_ is okay in God's eyes, then we can safely conclude that it must be okay to _borrow_ from the one who is doing the lending – or otherwise He wouldn't have given guidelines on lending.

Jesus doesn't condemn borrowing either, because in the Sermon on the Mount He says _"When they want to borrow money, lend it to them"_[4]. We need to be clear from the outset that it's not a sin to borrow money. If we are feeling guilty about being in debt, even when it is the result of our own foolishness, we can be set free because Jesus took the whole of our guilt on Himself on the Cross[5]. If _you_ are feeling guilty about your debt, talk to God about it in prayer so you can walk in the freedom the Cross brings.

Just because borrowing money is permissible in God's sight doesn't mean we should necessarily do it[6]. God's best for His people is that they should be the ones doing the lending – not the borrowing[7]. That's what it means to be the head and not the tail – which includes the area of finances we're looking at[8]. Once we're in a position to lend money to others, we need to be careful to follow God's guidelines. There a number of scriptures where we're directed by God not to charge interest, particularly if we're lending to the poor, or other Christians[9]. The only time we're permitted to charge interest on a loan is if we lend to those who are outside God's family[10].

The subject of lending money is a great example to show how the Kingdom of God and the world system are poles apart. When we look at the financial institutions operating in the world, they lend money in order to make a profit – that's why they exist. They're set up to take advantage of people's need to borrow money and then charge interest so they themselves can prosper. Some are so unscrupulous they will charge exorbitant interest rates, knowing there are some who are in such dire financial straits their only hope is to pay these inflated rates. The whole world system is geared around the financial institutions making more and more profit, at the expense of those who have no option but to borrow. Rarely, if at all will a financial establishment lend money purely for compassionate reasons.

God's system is completely the opposite. The reason God allows borrowing is because He has compassion for the poor. He understands the poor will need to borrow, and so He forbids the lender from charging interest because He doesn't want the poor to be exploited. God has a genuine compassion for the needy, and has therefore included certain checks and balances in His system to protect those who are most vulnerable. Zero percent interest rates is one of those checks. Not only does God's financial system protect the most vulnerable, he even goes a step further by saying that we need to keep a good attitude if we don't get our money back! If we can do that, we're demonstrating our Father's nature and character[11]. Any time that may happen to us, we won't be out of pocket because God has promised to be their Guarantor. If the poor can't pay us back, God promises He will[12]. That sounds like a good deal! Even though borrowing is not sinful, let's move on to see why being in debt is not God's best for us.

Practical Exercise

Make a list of 5 words that best describe your current financial situation. (e.g. 'trapped'; 'burdened' etc.).

Make a note of them below:

1.

2.

3.

4.

5.

2

The Truth About Debt

The Bible tells us *"A rich person rules poor people, and <u>a borrower is a slave to a lender"</u>*[1]. What exactly does it mean when it says the borrower is the slave of the lender? If we look back in history slaves were regarded as *property* by their owners, and were treated as such. They were shown little mercy because in the eyes of their owner they were a commodity. Slaves were bound to the person who owned them and had few if any civil rights – that was the owner's way of making sure their own interests were protected.

Even though the bondage borrowing brings doesn't compare to the immeasurable suffering and cruelty of the slave trade, we can glean some principles that carry over to the practice of borrowing money. Those who borrow money are also regarded as a commodity by their 'owners' – the financial institutions. There is often a lack of mercy and compassion for the individual if they default on their payments – the lender's attitude is usually 'profit before person'. The lender's first priority will always be to protect their own interests – usually at the expense of the ones who are doing the borrowing.

The Hebrew word for 'slave' in the verse from Proverbs 22:7 (above) describes this bondage as someone who is in subjection (under the rule of) the one who lends[2]. Interestingly, the root of this Hebrew word carries the meaning *'to work for another / to serve another by labor'*, implying the borrower is 'working' for the lender[3]. This is so true of the person who borrows money at interest because in their effort to earn a living, a portion of their income goes straight to the lender. Effectively, they are working for someone's else's benefit and so don't get to fully enjoy the fruit of their own labor. They are bound to this arrangement until all the debt is paid.

The Hebrew word for 'borrower' in this verse (Proverbs 22:7) is also worthy of closer attention. In the original language it means to 'unite', or to 'twine' something together[4]. Many people can relate to this personally, feeling trapped because they're tied to the lender and cannot escape. This is how I felt before becoming debt-free. The reality is however that there is a way out, because God has a plan and a destiny for each one of us to become debt-free. I say this with confidence because it's what He promises in His Word, and Jill and I can personally testify to it as our experience. It's a place where the individual is no longer at the beck and call of financial institutions. Once we're debt-free, the only One we need to consult with regarding financial decisions is God. God's plan *does* involve paying off all our debts, because we need to honor the people we've borrowed from, but He will make the process quicker and easier for us once we've made the decision to commit our way forward to Him[5].

Borrowing Strangles God's Church

When an individual gives part of their income to a financial institution by way of interest payments, they end up with less at their own disposal. This means if they have God's heart to try to help others with their finances, they're disadvantaged in what they're able to do. So, paying interest not only directly affects the borrower, it also has the potential to indirectly affect those whom God is asking us to help. The interest the borrower is paying to the lender is a 'stolen blessing' for one person or another – either for the borrower themselves, or for the person they may want to help in some way.

There is another side to this coin we also need to appreciate. Not only are we missing out by not being able to help others, we're actually giving it to someone else to do what they want with it. Some financial institutions have a low social and ethical conscience, so our interest payments may be paying for their poor practices. If we haven't done any homework on the ethical values of the lender we're borrowing from, we may be indirectly sponsoring certain activities and organizations without knowing. In a way, paying interest is a double-whammy – we're held back from not being able to use the money in the way we would like to, yet at the same time we're potentially financing an organization to use it in ways that violate Biblical values.

Borrowing money has the potential to curtail God's call on an individual's life. Being tied to the lender means we are not 'free agents' to respond to a direction the Lord may be leading us in, so it will be the Gospel that eventually suffers. This can be extremely frustrating for the individual who is sensing God's call but isn't able to freely respond. *The good news is that no matter what bondage we may be experiencing in the area of finances, God can bring us out of it.* As long as we totally commit our way to Him and trust His way forward, nothing can ultimately stop our God given destiny - not even financial debt.

Borrowing Brings Responsibilities

For those times we do decide to borrow money, the Bible is clear regarding the attitude we should take. To start with, we need to make sure we don't rush into a debt agreement.

Proverbs tells us *"Careful planning leads to profit. Acting too quickly leads to poverty"*[6]. The sorts of questions we should be asking ourselves before taking out a loan are: *"Have I heard God on this? Is there any other way I can do what I need to do without borrowing money? Do I really need this item now, or can I wait and save to buy it?"*. These are sensible questions to ask ourselves before committing to taking out a loan.

We're also warned not to offer ourselves as guarantors for other people's debt. Proverbs again tells us we shouldn't promise to pay someone else's debt, because if they default and we end up not being able to pay, we'll end up losing what we have – even the bed we sleep on![7] Then there's the matter of actually keeping our word and making sure we repay what we owe. There's no way of sugar coating this, but the Bible calls those who borrow and end up not paying their debt as *wicked*[8]. In a Biblical sense the 'wicked' are guilty of a crime; they are guilty of sinning against God, as well as the person they have borrowed from[9].

Borrowing is Not a Blessing

The promise that God's people would be the lenders, not the borrowers, is listed in the *blessings* that God has spoken over His people[10]. Nowhere in the Bible is debt referred to as a blessing, in fact the opposite is true - debt is actually listed as one of the *curses* in Deuteronomy 28:15-68. In verses 43 & 44 we're told *"Foreigners living among you shall become richer and richer while you become poorer and poorer. They shall lend to you, not you to them! They shall be the head and you shall be the tail!"*[11]

Before anyone gets carried away to think their debt is the result of being cursed, let me bring a word of reassurance. When our faith is in Christ, the reason we're in debt is not because we're cursed, but because we haven't yet taken a full hold of the blessing! Because of what Christ has done and our faith in Him, we are *completely* redeemed from the curse – which includes financial lack.

The Law stated that anyone who is hung on a tree is cursed[12], which means that Jesus became a curse as He hung on the tree (the Cross) at Calvary. The Apostle Paul gives us insight into this, explaining that through this sacrificial act, God was redeeming those who put their faith in Him *from* the curse, so they can *receive* the blessing[13]. Put very simply, the curse pronounced in Deuteronomy 28:43-44 has no validity in the life of the person who has their faith in Christ. That person becomes a 'non-stick pan' to *every* curse because of what Christ has done on their behalf!

Let me say it again, as followers of Christ our debt is not because we're cursed, but because we haven't yet fully taken hold of the blessing that is ours in Christ[14]. This book is written to help the individual journey towards the blessing of being financially free, so let's move on to look at the next step.

Practical Exercise

How ethical are the organizations you are borrowing from? Do some research to make sure you are in agreement with their values. If you're not in agreement, start praying and asking for guidance regarding what you should do.

3

God Our Provider

In the Old Testament, God introduced Himself to Abraham as 'Almighty God' ('*El-Shadday*')[1]. By using this title, God was not only describing Himself as great and mighty, He was also revealing Himself as the One who could supply all of Abraham's needs. In the original Hebrew language, the word for *Almighty* describes God as the One who has an unlimited supply of resources, and that He is generous with what He has[2]. It's one thing to have plenty, it's another to be generous with it. God has both attributes – the abundance of goodness and grace, as well as a generous heart to go with it. By presenting Himself as *El–Shadday*, God was offering to meet all of Abraham's spiritual, emotional, as well as physical (material) needs. As we follow Abraham in the book of Genesis, we see how this became a reality in his life[3].

No one name can reveal the full character and nature of God, which is why God went on to reveal Himself by other names as well throughout the Old Testament. Each of these names reveals a different facet of God's nature and character. One of these other names is *Yehôvâh Yir'eh*, which means *"The LORD Will Provide"*[4]. This name was revealed to Abraham on Mount Moriah when, as he was about to sacrifice his son Isaac the Lord stepped in to provide a ram for the sacrifice[5].

There are a number of things the name "The LORD Will Provide" ('*Yehôvâh Yir'eh*') tells us about the nature and character of God. The Hebrew meaning of this name means 'to see' – which points to how God 'sees' a need in advance and then makes sure the provision for that need is in place. This is exactly what happened at Mount Moriah – God saw Abraham's need for a sacrifice and provided the ram. But there is a deeper significance to this account as well, because it was pointing ahead to when God would provide another sacrifice – His Son Jesus on Calvary. Jesus' sacrifice is the result of God 'looking ahead' and seeing mankind's need for a sacrifice to atone for their sin. Jesus is God's provision, the 'Lamb of God' who takes away the sin of the world[6]. The English translation 'The LORD Will Provide' is consistent with the Hebrew meaning because it conveys God's *pro-vision* for His people. *'Pro'* as a prefix means 'forward / in advance / beforehand'; and *'vision'* is 'to see'.

What About Us?

> *"So all who put their faith in Christ share the same blessing*
> *Abraham received because of his faith"*
> *(Galatians 3:9 NLT)*

It's one thing to look at how God revealed Himself to a Biblical giant like Abraham, but it's another to have the confidence He will do the same for us. Does God relate to us in the same way He did to Abraham? In the verse above the apostle Paul says He does, so let's briefly explore why Paul is able to say this.

If we go back to how God revealed Himself to Abraham as *'El-Shadday'*[7], what's important to realize is the promise was also to Abraham's *descendants*[8]. The Apostle Paul tells us that *all* who have their faith in Jesus Christ are descendants of Abraham, because it is *through faith in Christ* that an individual comes into the family, not through natural lineage![9] Becoming a 'son of Abraham' through faith in Christ positions the believer to receive all the blessings Abraham enjoyed, because God's promise included his descendants!

When our faith is in Christ, God promises to bountifully provide all we need, in the same way He provided for Abraham's needs. The promise is for every material, emotional, spiritual, and financial need we may have[10]. *"Since he did not spare even his own Son for us but gave him up for us all, won't he also surely give us everything else?"* (Romans 8:32 TLB). God, by His very nature is a Provider – it's what the names *El-Shadday* and *Yehôvâh Yir'eh* reveal. It's who He is – it's in His DNA - that's good news for all who put their faith in Christ!

Provision is More Than Material

God doesn't just want to meet our material needs - He wants to meet our emotional and spiritual needs as well. When God gives Himself to us in Christ, He becomes the love we're looking for, the peace we desire, and the security we need. God wants us to come to know Him as the *Person* He is, not just as someone who will provide materially for us. Our motivation to seek God needs to be driven by the desire to get to know Him for who He is, not what He can give us materially. When our priority is to seek His face first[11], rather than His hand, we'll find His material provision will follow, because it's in His nature to provide.

Having only our financial needs met by God (or any other source) is not the answer to living a contented life. Becoming debt-free makes life easier, but it doesn't fill the void in our hearts because the void is spiritual. Jesus said *"no one can live only on food. People need every word that God has spoken"*[12]. He's quoting from the Old Testament[13], saying material things alone will never satisfy because we need the spiritual life that comes from hearing God's voice. It's only as we get to know God's *heart*, through a relationship with Jesus Christ that we find the true fulfilment we're looking for in life. Debt-freedom can't bring that life, so if we limit our relationship with Him to only seeking His financial provision, we'll miss out on everything else. He wants us to experience *all of Him* - His love, His security, His peace, as well as His joy (to mention a few). These are the things that truly make us alive, not simply having our financial needs met.

Finding ourselves experiencing the love, joy, and peace of God is the abundant life Jesus promised[14]. Knowing God in Jesus Christ and experiencing His grace brings us to that place – a place where 'rivers of living water' rise up to give us the peace and fulfilment that material things can't bring[15]. So let's be careful to make sure we're seeking Him *for who He is* as our first priority, seeking Him for the Person He is, not simply for what He can give materially. As we do, it won't be long before we experience His hand opening up to us as well[16].

The Promise of Provision

Jesus taught how God cares for us, and how His provision comes out of a heart of love towards us. Having our needs met by God is not a formula – it is the manifestation of God's love and goodness. For that reason, Jesus tells us not to worry about the material things we need in order to live, because God already knows we need them[17].

To illustrate His point, Jesus tells us God feeds the 'birds of the air' even though they don't do anything to earn it. He then goes on to say if God feeds them, despite not putting any effort into their own provision, how much more will He look after *us* when we are far more valuable to Him than birds[18]. Similarly, the clothes we wear. Jesus paints a picture of how the 'lilies of the field' grow to become beautiful, even though once again, they don't contribute to the process. Solomon in all his splendor didn't compare to how glorious they look. If God is willing to clothe something as transient as lilies, Jesus is reassuring us God will clothe us, because we are far more valuable to Him![19]

Unlike the birds of the air and the lilies of the field we do need to work![20.] In His teaching, Jesus contrasts the lowly, temporary things with the highly valued (us); but also contrasts things that don't work (birds and lilies), with those who do (us). It's as if Jesus is saying *"Surely you can see how, if God is faithful in providing for menial temporary things who don't lift a finger, you can understand how God will absolutely provide for those He regards as far more valuable, especially considering they're willing to work!"*

There is a clause in what Jesus promises regarding the Father's faithfulness to provide, because He says *"But seek (aim at and strive after) first of all His kingdom and His righteousness (His way of doing and being right), and then all these things taken together will be given you besides"*[21]. Jesus knows we need more than our material needs met. He knows that life – the abundant life He came to give[22] is where we'll find our peace and security. That's why He is telling us to make it our priority to seek God's Kingdom *first*, effectively pointing us in the direction of where we'll find the abundant life He came to give.

He Is a Good Father

Jesus gives us further insight into God's heart as a Provider when He shares how good a Father God is. Jesus asked those who were listening what sort of an earthly father would give his child a stone, when the child asked for a loaf. Similarly, what sort of father would give a snake when the child asked for a fish. Any father who loves their child wouldn't dream of doing such a thing! The point Jesus is making is this, if earthly fathers don't act this way even though they're imperfect, *how much more* will God in Heaven, who is perfect, give good gifts to those who ask Him![23]

It is possible that our earthly father has made it difficult for us to relate to God as a loving, caring Father. If we've had a childhood where we've not been nurtured in love, or have suffered at the hands of an abusive and cruel father, it makes it difficult for us to relate to what Jesus is saying. It's in situations like this we need to simply trust that Jesus knows what He's talking about. Even though we may not have personally experienced God as a loving Father yet, Jesus has, because Jesus knew God the Father personally.

Jesus knew exactly what God was like[24], which means He's talking from *experience*, not a theory or a philosophy. We need to trust Jesus and take Him at His Word – and believe that God won't let us down. When we do that, it is a vital step to allowing God to reveal Himself to us for who He truly is. We will eventually be able to testify from our *experience* He is a good Father, in the same way Jesus could.

God is a Provider by nature - it's who He is. He's kind and generous with the abundance He has. This is what He revealed to Abraham, promising to do the same for his descendants. Jesus tells us God is the perfect loving Father who only gives good gifts to His children – which includes material and financial provision. This is the God who is offering Himself to us now in the Person Jesus Christ. All He asks us to do is to trust Him and put Him first – to seek Him as our life's priority until we find the truth and our fulfilment in Him. Then Jesus' experience will become *our* experience, and we too will know God as the perfect Father who is faithful in all His provision.

1. Ask yourself whether seeking *'God's Kingdom and His righteousness'* is your first priority in life. Be honest with yourself because there's a lot at stake. Ask God to help you, and to show you any steps you may need to take. Make a record of them if it helps.

2. Make a list of 5 words or phrases that best describe where you _would like to get to_ with regard to your financial situation. Make a note of them below: (Habakkuk 2:2-3)

1.

2.

3.

4.

5.

4

God Is Bigger Than Our Debt

Financial debt can be daunting, but it's no match for God. As we look at the debt we have, it may try to intimidate us in the same way Goliath tried to intimidate David. Even though the enemy was threatening him, David stood firm in the Lord, and then brought down his enemy[1]. David's secret was very simple – he recognized the fight was primarily *spiritual*, not physical. He declared to Goliath *"You come to me with a sword, a spear, and a javelin, but I come to you in the name of the Lord of hosts, the God of the armies of Israel, whom you have taunted"*[2]. Goliath's size, his armor, and the weapons he was carrying must have made him a terrifying sight, but despite what he saw in the natural, David declared he had a greater weapon – *"the name of the Lord of hosts, the God of the armies of Israel"*. David had a faith and a confidence in the spiritual weapon he had been given - *'the name of the Lord God Almighty'*[3].

Someone's *name* is their *reputation*, so David's hope of victory was in the One he knew to be faithful in keeping His promises[4]. Even though David was the one on the front line facing this enemy, he knew it was actually God who would be doing the fighting[5]. David was confident of victory because he knew God was faithful and right beside him in the fight, and so didn't allow the taunts of the enemy to distract him. David's part was to stand firm, use the name of the Lord, and make sure he didn't allow what he saw in the natural to intimidate him.

We need to have the same attitude towards our debt as David did Goliath, because our debt may feel like we're facing a giant. The *total* debt we owe can be compared to the whole of the Philistine army trying to defeat the Israelites, then amongst the army there is one 'giant'. For most people the giant is their mortgage. Even in the absence of a large debt like a mortgage, there is usually one debt that stands out above the rest. Like Goliath, it will try to intimidate and threaten the individual – taunting them with "what if's". *'What if I lose my job?' 'What will happen to the house if I get ill and can't pay my bills?'* All these things may be real possibilities, but the enemy will use them to try to steal our peace and faith in God, in the same way Goliath tried to steal David's confidence in God[6].

No enemy, no matter how big, was a match for God's people in the account of David and Goliath, because they had the Lord on their side. No financial debt, whether big or small, will be a match for us providing we take on David's attitude – a faith and confidence in God and His promises. Once we know God is on our side, nothing can stop us. Once we understand God is fighting our battles for us[7], it's not a case of 'if', but 'when' the giant will fall. We'll be looking at the issue of confronting the mortgage in more detail later in the book.

The Fight of Faith

Our battle with the giant of financial debt is not fought in a valley in Judah like David's was[8] - our battle is fought between our ears – in our minds. The 'natural man' will fight us by bringing negative thoughts and anxieties, especially when we hear or read bad reports about the economy, or if our job is under threat. The aim of this sort of intimidation is to try to stop us believing we can become debt-free, despite God promising we can[9].

It doesn't take much effort for the natural mind to believe that one day we'll be free from our mortgage. Our minds can understand how the process of paying a monthly fee, over a set period of time (as set out in the mortgage agreement) will eventually pay off the mortgage. But believing we can become debt-free *supernaturally* with God, quicker than the natural process of events, is where the challenge lies. We may believe God can do it, but our natural mind will want to understand *how* He will do it. That's why faith is needed whenever we're believing God for anything – a faith and trust in His Word even though we don't understand with our natural mind[10]. Though we may believe with our *spirit* God can do it, (with our heart), our *natural mind* (flesh) will try to oppose what we believe because its 'modus operandi' is senses, not faith[11]. This opposition is the outworking of the battle between the flesh and the Spirit, a battle that all who follow Christ are familiar with as they seek to remain faithful to His Word[12].

The time when things look impossible is the time to stand and fight – just like David did. At a time when the hope of victory seemed farcical, as much as it did impossible, David stood in faith in the name of the Lord and overturned the odds by killing Goliath. When those seemingly impossible situations arise for us – whether it's in the area of finances or anything else - those are the times when we need to *"Let heaven fill your thoughts; don't spend your time worrying about things down here"*. (Colossians 3:2 (TLB). The fight of faith is not easy – that's why it's called a *'fight'*[13] – but we have a path to victory when we make sure we don't dwell on what we can see in the natural (our bank balance, credit card statement etc.) – but to fix our gaze on what God is saying in His Word. That's the front line of the battle, and that's where the victory is eventually won.

We've Been Given the Ability to Choose

The times when the flesh is bombarding us with negative thoughts and emotions are the times we need to make a willful choice regarding what we believe[14]. Despite what our emotions may be telling us through the circumstances we're looking at, we have a free will, given to us by God, to choose what we want to believe. Will we believe God's promises, or is there a danger we'll stagger and believe only what our flesh is saying as it interprets things through the senses? We're not denying what our bank statement is saying, but by believing God in His Word we're inviting a higher truth into our situation – a truth that has the power to change what is 'facts'[15]. It's the times we're willing to *"Look straight ahead, and fix our eyes on what lies before us"*[16] that will take us forward on our journey of faith towards debt-freedom, even if our steps are small to start with. As we give less and less attention to what our circumstances are saying, and at the same time give more and more attention to what God is promising, our faith will grow and we'll become increasingly confident God will do it.

We're Participators, Not Spectators

David had to play his part in bringing down Goliath. We too have to play our part in bringing down our financial debt – both spiritually, and practically. David used his *spiritual* weapon first (the name of the Lord), then followed it up with his *physical* weapon – the sling and a smooth stone[17]. The *spiritual* part of seeing victory for us is just as important, if not more important than the *practical* part (budgeting etc.) – and needs to come first. The battle is ultimately God's, but if we lean on Him with all our heart, He will walk us through and build us up in faith, as well as give us wisdom to exercise good practices[18]. As we choose to believe what He has promised in

His Word first and foremost, and then trust His ability (His power) to do what He's promised, wisdom comes to help us make the practical adjustments that take us towards debt-freedom.

God's Perspective Is 'Above and Beyond'

"With God's power working in us, he can do much, much more than anything we can ask or think of"
Ephesians 3:20 (ERV)

If we're willing to ask God to help us become debt-free, He will do it. He will actually do more than what we ask - that's what the verse above is promising us. Whatever financial debt we may have – credit cards, loans, bills, even our mortgage – not only can God help us clear it, He can take us further. We often struggle to believe we'll ever be debt-free because debt is all we've ever known, but God doesn't have the same struggle because He can see outside of the box we're trapped in. Seeing us in financial freedom is a case of "His thoughts being higher than our thoughts"[19] - He can see it even when we can't. We are privileged however, because He invites us into the place where we can also see it – a place where the Holy Spirit reveals to us God's perspective[20]. That's the place of faith, where we see God's promises from His Word, with the Holy Spirit illuminating the promise to us and giving us faith to believe. Once that happens the fight is on – the 'good fight of faith' to hold on to the promise God has spoken to us in the Word, despite the opposition from the flesh.

If you're struggling to believe God can clear your debt – for whatever reason – spend time looking at your situation from God's perspective. Take time to look at, read, and meditate on what God says in His Word regarding your needs – especially your financial needs as you look to become debt-free. Build yourself a picture of how God sees your situation, not what your natural senses are painting for you through what you see, read, and hear on the news, or what your latest credit card or bank statement may be trying to tell you. What it says on the news about the economy is not bigger than God. What you read on your credit card statement is not bigger than God. Neither is what the enemy is telling you through your negative thoughts, bigger than God.

Foolishness Is Not a Barrier

If our debt is the result of being foolish, there's an easy solution – we need to stop being foolish. Whatever part foolishness may have played in getting us to the place we're at now, it cannot stop us moving forward as long as we make the choice not to remain foolish. Foolishness is simply a lack of wisdom[21] – it's a lack of not knowing what the right thing to do is at the right time. The antidote to foolishness is wisdom, because by definition the person who takes wisdom on board will not remain foolish any longer. That's why we're strongly urged by God to seek wisdom as a life priority[22]. Wisdom shouts loudly, and so is easy to find[23]. Wisdom is a person – the Lord Jesus Christ, and it's as we spend time in the Bible under the direction of the Holy Spirit, we hear Wisdom speaking to us – sometimes loudly and clearly, other times softly, with a small still voice[24]. Not only will Wisdom reveal and then cement the will of God to us in our hearts as we spend time digging into the Bible, Wisdom will also give us practical insight, helping us navigate the path that takes us towards debt freedom. Let's make sure we respond to Wisdom's invitation to help us, and not allow foolishness to guide us one step further on our journey.

1. Make a list of the total debt you owe on a piece of notebook. Include the name of the creditors and the amount you owe them. Add the amounts together to get a total figure. *Once you've done that, fold the piece of paper in half (with the writing on the inside).* Start countering the intimidation you may be feeling in your thoughts and emotions by writing out 1 Samuel 17:45-46 on the outside. You may need to look at various Bible translations before deciding on a translation that resonates with you. Put the piece of paper in a prominent place and continue confessing on a regular basis what the scriptures say about your debt. Declare that although it may appear to be a giant, it's coming down in the Name of Jesus.

5

No Other God

We read in the Bible how a young man ran up to Jesus and knelt before Him[1]. We're told this was someone who was extremely wealthy[2], influential[3], and religious. This would have been somebody who was well known and respected in the synagogue, because no Jew who can say they've kept the commandments from their youth, as this man did[4], would have missed attendance on the Sabbath. There was a great deal of personal risk for a devout Jew like this to bow before Jesus and call Him "Good Teacher"[5]. In acknowledging Jesus so publicly, he was putting himself in danger of being expelled from the synagogue. With that would come the loss of reputation, as well as the respect he had built up over many years.

Despite his wealth and position of authority, and despite his religious zeal, he knew there was something missing in his life – which is why he came to look for Jesus. The awareness of 'there must be more to life than this' was so strong in him that he was willing to risk everything, believing he would find it in Jesus. He wasn't wrong, but sadly he walks away empty handed, lacking the very thing he was prepared to risk everything for[6]. What went wrong for him?

The question he asks Jesus is *"what shall I do to inherit eternal life"*[7]. Jesus replies with a list of commandments, to which the young man answers he's kept them all[8]. Jesus wasn't pointing to the commandments suggesting they were the means to receiving eternal life, because eternal life is a gift, received through faith in Christ as a result of God's grace[9]. Jesus was simply trying to help this religious young man see something he hadn't yet seen for himself.

The man thought he was obeying all the commandments, but Jesus tried to help him see how he'd actually failed at the first hurdle - *"You shall have no other gods before Me"*[10]. By telling him to sell all he had and give it to the poor, Jesus was showing him the 'other god' he had in his life[11]. His wealth had become his security, it's what his life was built on, and it's where he saw his future hopes being fulfilled. Jesus loved this man[12] and knew he was genuinely seeking God. He wanted to help him see the idol he had made of money by challenging him to let go of it, before inviting him to give God first place in his heart by following Him (Jesus).

Sadly, the young man walked away. I believe this to be one of the saddest accounts in Jesus' ministry. This young man came face to face with God in the flesh, and was given an invitation to have a relationship with Him ('follow Me'). Yet he turned away, all because money had a hold on him to the extent he wasn't prepared to let go of it to follow Jesus.

What About Us?

This is a stark warning regarding the real threat that exists in having a wrong relationship with money. This includes those who regard themselves as already following Christ, as well as those who are currently outside the Kingdom - as this young man was. Jesus is clear in His teaching about the dangers of having a wrong relationship with money. He says *"No one can serve two masters at the same time. You will hate one of them and love the other. Or you will be faithful to one and dislike the other. You can't serve God and money at the same time."*[13] We have to make our mind up where our devotion lies - is it with God, or is it in riches? We can't have a foot in both camps - Jesus makes this very clear. Neither does Jesus give us the option of being indifferent and not having to choose. We have to make a choice on this issue - whether it is Christ who has first place in our hearts, or money.

The hold money has on some people is very strong, making it extremely difficult to make the choice of putting God first in their lives. Though I can empathize with this, it's not possible to avoid having to make the choice if we want God's best for our lives. To help us make the right decision, Jesus even tells us the option we should go for - *"What you should want most is God's kingdom and doing what he wants you to do. Then he will give you all these other things you need."*[14] If we read the verse in context, 'all these other things you need' refers to our material needs[15] - as we've already seen in a previous chapter. So here is Jesus teaching us the dangers of serving two masters; challenging us to make a choice[16]; explaining how God knows we need food and clothing[17]; before finishing off by telling us if we choose God's Kingdom first, we'll get those things aswell![18] Jesus has laid out the truth before us. It's then up to us to make the choice whether we trust what He's saying by taking the step of faith to make the Kingdom of God our priority.

Money Is Not Evil

A knife can be used as an instrument for good, or for evil. The same knife can be used to prepare a meal to feed those who are experiencing homelessness, or it can be used to injure someone, even killing them. *It's not the knife that's the problem, but what a person chooses to do with the knife.* It's the same principle with money - a person can use money to stop someone from being evicted from their home because of arrears, or it can be used to hire a 'hit man' to kill someone. Money in and of itself is neither good nor evil - it is neutral - *it is what people choose to do with money* that determines whether it's an instrument of good, or evil.

A verse that's often misunderstood, and then misquoted is 1 Timothy 6:10. We may even have misquoted it ourselves by saying "money is the root of all evil". But that's not what the verse says. What the verse *actually* says is "the <u>love</u> of money is the root of all evil" - which is a completely different thing. It's the <u>love</u> of money, where a person gives first place in their heart to money that is the root of all evil - not the money itself.

The root system is what feeds a growing plant. The 'love of money' is called the 'root' of all evil because it feeds all the other areas of an individual's life. The love of money will feed the deception that money can bring fulfilment and a satisfied life - when the Bible tells us it can't[19]. Solomon shares this wisdom with us - *"If you love money and wealth, you will never be satisfied with what you have"*[20]. He knew first-hand what he was talking about because he was the wealthiest king Israel has ever known. No matter how much money a person has, the love of money will make them carry on looking for more because they will never be satisfied with what they have. A love for money shapes everything about an individual's life - their time and energy will be spent on getting, accumulating, and then spending money. This is what Jesus meant when He said *"Your heart will always be where your treasure is"*[21]. Our heart always follows what we value most, which in turn will reflect how we live our lives, what our priorities are, including how we treat other people.

It is a deception to believe that riches can bring fulfilment, because enjoying life to the full, 'until it overflows' can only be found in Jesus[22]. If it could be found anywhere else then there would have been no need for Jesus to come and suffer as He did[23]. The love of money is extremely dangerous because it 'chokes' the Word of God - it will stop faith growing in our hearts when we read the Bible, eventually causing us to fall away[24]. That's when God's Kingdom is relegated to second, third or even fourth place in a person's life, and they end up missing the abundant life Jesus came to give.

The Amplified Bible for 1 Timothy 6:10 is an excellent summary of the dangers a love for money can bring, when it says: *"For the love of money [that is, the greedy desire for it and the willingness to gain it unethically] is a root of all sorts of evil, and some by longing for it have wandered away from the faith and pierced themselves [through and through] with many sorrows." - 1 Timothy 6:10 (AMP).* Giving first place in our hearts to money rather than God is what happened to the rich young ruler, and he paid the ultimate price for it. His love of money blinded him from seeing the value of the One who was inviting him to receive the eternal life he was so desperate to find. He fell for the deception, and ended up forfeiting his soul[25].

Let me remind the reader once more that money is neutral - it is neither good nor evil - it is the _love_ of money, an unhealthy attitude of the heart towards money, that is the wolf dressed up in sheep's clothing. It is a wicked influence that will try to steal everything God is offering us - even our eternal destiny. The sobering thing is that it is *our responsibility* to make sure we are free from the love of money[26] - it doesn't happen 'by chance'. It is our responsibility alone whether we choose God or Mammon as our heart's desire - nobody else's.

Heart Attitude is Key

The Bible doesn't warn us against having money - it warns us about the dangers of having *a wrong relationship* with money. The good news for the Christian is that it's possible to have a *right relationship* with money. This is a relationship where we're using money for good, not for evil - using it for righteous purposes, not unrighteous. It's the place where money doesn't have a hold on our hearts - we're the ones calling the shots with regard to money - not the other way round. When we're in that place, we know that God is our Master, and money has now become our *slave*. It's the place where we tell money what to do, not the other way around. It's the place where we seek God's leading as to where and how we spend our money, rather than money controlling us through fear of lack, selfishness, or greed.

A wrong relationship with money is the result of not having a right relationship with God. If we give our attention to building a right relationship with God, the danger of having a wrong relationship with money will diminish. Building our relationship with God will help us appreciate how precious He is, to the point where nothing else we desire compares with the Treasure we see in Him[27].

In the parable of the talents[28], the man with one talent had a completely wrong image of his master. In his mind, his master was a hard taskmaster, not willing to give, yet expecting much[29]. This led him to act fearfully, ending up burying the talent he'd been given[30]. If he'd have taken the time to get to know his master, he would have realized he was generous, encouraging, and joyful[31], which in turn would have given him the freedom and confidence to make a different choice.

Seeking the Kingdom of God means we seek to know God better. It means building our relationship with Him, and as we do that it becomes the antidote to having a wrong relationship with money. Seeking His heart and His ways will protect us from the love of money and the empty promises it brings. As we get to know the heart of the One we've surrendered our lives to, He Himself will teach us to trust Him for our provision, as well as give us generous hearts that reflect His nature to the world around us[32].

The parable of the talents also demonstrates that *the amount* of money we have is not the issue, but reinforces *it's our relationship* with how much we've got that's under scrutiny. It's possible to have a wrong relationship with money even if we've only got a little - as this man with one talent demonstrated. Despite having a little, he was still judged by his master because he used the little he had incorrectly. If we currently see ourselves as the man with one talent, let's make sure we don't take on his attitude. Let's seek God's heart as our priority, let's make sure building our relationship with Him is our primary focus. Out of that comes a wisdom to know how to correctly use what we've got - even if it's only a little to start with.

What if I Have a Wrong Relationship with Money?

If you see evidence in your own life suggesting you may have drifted into a wrong relationship with money, the good news is that it doesn't have to continue. It's possible to do something about it - even today. The first thing to do is to thank God for showing you. The uneasiness you've been feeling regarding this issue is the indicator God wants to take you to a better place.

Thank Him for His mercy, that He loves you unconditionally and does not want to see you being *"pierced through with many sorrows"*[33] by continuing on the path you're on.

Secondly, you need to repent. Go to God and apologize for your actions and attitudes. Admit you were wrong. Ask and then receive His forgiveness[34]. When we humble ourselves like this, it opens the door for God to draw near to us. He will take the opportunity to give us His grace (strength) to go forward, as well as take us on to better things in Him[35].

Thirdly, choose God as your Master *as a decision of the heart -* then confess it with your mouth. When we've made a decision in our hearts, and then confess it with our mouths, something happens in the spiritual realm. Heart and mouth in agreement are a powerful weapon[36].

Then finally, surrender to the Holy Spirit and ask Him to guide you, as well as strengthen you in your relationship with Christ. We have been given the Holy Spirit so we can know the truth[37], which happens as He leads us into a deeper relationship with Jesus[38]. It's as we get to know Him and our relationship with Him strengthens, that money will become less and less attractive to us - because He will be the One who is at the center of our life.

Take some time to write down how you would describe your relationship with money at the moment. Does it consume you, or are you indifferent towards it? Secondly, write down how you would describe your relationship with God. How do they compare? Do you need to make some adjustments to redress the balance? If you do, recognize it's a heart issue and take some time to look at the steps outlined at the end of the chapter.

6

Working with God

God's objective is not limited to helping us become debt-free. God also wants us to change our thinking so He can take us to a place where we have an excess of finances to help others. Proverbs 23:7 tells us, what we believe in our hearts is reflected in our outward life: *"For as he thinks within himself, so he is"*. This means a person's financial situation is a reflection of what they believe about money, so unless the person who is in debt changes their thinking, they will remain in debt. This change in the way they think is what the Bible calls *"the renewal of the mind"*[1]. It simply means getting rid of old ways of thinking, and taking on board God's way of thinking, which He reveals to us through His Word. There are areas in all of our lives where we need to ask the Holy Spirit to help us renew our minds so we can think the way God thinks, including the area of finance. The apostle Paul says it like this: *"…let God change you inside with a new way of thinking. Then you will be able to understand and accept what God wants for you"*[2]. To move to the place of becoming debt-free in God, we have to align ourselves with the way He thinks, which He freely shares with us in His Word.

I shared earlier how on our journey to becoming debt-free, I was hoping there would be a one-time event where Jill and I would be given all the money we needed to clear our debts. On reflection, that wouldn't have brought us the longer-term benefits we're now experiencing, because without a change in our *thinking*, we would have slipped back to where we were.

We would have continued in the same foolish and undisciplined ways, so our debt-freedom would likely have been short lived.

Getting to the place of becoming debt-free is a journey rather than a one-time event. Yes, there is a point on the journey when we experience the joy and relief of finally paying off our last debt, but in getting to that place we have to realize that our thinking regarding money has to change. Having our minds renewed on the way is as important as the actual experience of becoming debt-free. Without it, there is a danger we'll slip back into debt, because we won't have learnt the Biblical principles of stewardship.

It's on the journey towards debt-freedom that our minds are renewed to understand how God views finances. It's on the journey we start to appreciate we have certain responsibilities if we're going to see debt freedom become a reality in our lives. The option to put all the responsibility on God to bring us into debt-freedom is not available to us. We have *to work with God* to become debt-free - asking Him to teach us from His Word how He views finances, as well as asking Him to give us the wisdom we need to use what we've got in the way He intended. If we're not familiar with God's ways of dealing with finances we'll be led by the flesh, which can be dangerous because it leads to either self-gratification at one end of the spectrum, or being tight-fisted on the other. A heart taught by God will reflect the One who is teaching them[3]. Their security will not be in money, nor will they be slow to be generous with what they have.

A failure to engage with God through His Word in the area of finances means the individual will remain in the same place. It is the place where they're not able to steward money correctly and so become increasingly frustrated because they're not seeing much progress. There's also an unsettling awareness that they're falling short of the fulness of what God has planned for them. On the other hand, *working with God*, which comes through opening our hearts to the Holy Spirit will bring loving correction, wisdom, and an understanding of God's way of doing things. This in turn brings self-discipline and good stewardship so that the individual can move forward. They will not only be making progress towards debt-freedom, they will also be positioning themselves for God to be able to trust them with more of His riches, both spiritually and materially[4].

Jesus said something remarkable when He said *"If you cannot be trusted with worldly riches, you will not be trusted with the true riches"*[5]. He made it clear that showing ourselves as trustworthy in the area of finances sets us up for God to trust us with *true* riches, which are the secrets of His Kingdom. Conversely, a failure to handle finances in the right way stops us from receiving the fulness of what God wants us to have. Making sure we handle money in a Biblical way is therefore essential for us. We need to get it right so that we will receive all of what God has planned for us.

God Does Not Discriminate

We can sometimes look at other Christians and think because they are financially better off than we are, God favors them more than us. It's a mistake to think like this because God doesn't show favoritism[6]. What is true however is that God blesses individuals in line with what they are able to handle. In the parable of the talents which we looked at earlier, the master distributed his wealth according to the individual's *ability*, not because of favoritism[7]. He gave five talents to one man because he was confident he would use them wisely, which proved to be correct when he came back to settle accounts[8].

51

It's common sense really - would we entrust our money to someone who will deal with it wisely, or foolishly? God's attitude is the same, but it's not simply a case of being concerned we'll squander His resources. He also understands how wealth, without the wisdom to know how to handle it, has the potential to ruin an individual.

Even though our current situation may reflect we've not been that good at handling money, there is hope! With God's help, we can change and be brought to a place where we can be trusted with more. Even the man who had ten talents didn't start off with ten. He started with five, and it was only as he demonstrated he could handle what he'd been given properly was he given more responsibility[9]. The master was right to give only a single talent to one man, because he didn't use it wisely. Even with one talent though, if he'd used it properly, he also would have been given more once he'd demonstrated he could steward the little he had.

No matter how much or how little we have, if we can prove we can handle what we already have correctly, increase will come. Even if we start at the place where we really have no clue how to handle finances, there is One who will help us. If we ask, and that's all we need to do as long as we're sincere, the Holy Spirit will teach us, guide us, and give us the wisdom we need to take us from where we are now, to the place where we're debt-free and then beyond. It's the place where we'll experience financial freedom, but equally important, it's a place where we'll be equipped to handle money in the right way.

Over and Above

It's very important to understand God is not looking to simply clear our debt and meet our needs. God is also looking to provide us with more than enough so we can have a surplus to help other people as well. For some, becoming debt-free and then settling down to a comfortable lifestyle is their main goal. This is not God's best for the individual, because God wants to take us further. He wants to take us *beyond* our own needs being met, to a place where we have enough to be generous to others as well.

It's selfish to settle in the place where only our own needs are met, with no desire to want more so we can meet other people's needs out of our excess. If we allow Him, the Holy Spirit will challenge our thinking by revealing to us God's heart. God's heart is to take us further down the road than having our own needs met. He wants us to reflect His heart where we're able to be generous to others out of our overflow. It's as our minds are renewed through the Word of God that we capture God's heart of generosity, a heart He is willing to give us so that we too can be generous towards others.

Everybody likes to receive a gift because it brings with it a sense of worth and appreciation. A gift is a statement of love from the giver. But Jesus says *"Giving gifts is more satisfying than receiving them"*[10]. It may be difficult for some to appreciate that giving brings more joy than receiving. *Giving* is where God's heart is, and so working with God in order for Him to change our heart to line up with His, will bring us to the place of experiencing the joy of giving. As we bless others with good gifts, as we show generosity and kindness, it displays the nature of who our Father is[11]. We become His hands and His feet, expressing here on earth the heart he has to bless those who are in need[12].

Becoming debt-free is not the end goal, it's just a milestone. Debt freedom is a staging-post on the way to something bigger that God wants to do in all of us. He wants to show His heart to the world around us in a practical way, a heart of love and kindness, a heart of generosity and thoughtfulness towards those who are in need. He is willing to give us the resources for us to be able to do this - but only if we have the wisdom to know how to deal with what we're given, as well as a heart that reflects His. He is willing to be the Source for us to be able to bless others, but we need to work with Him, allowing the Holy Spirit to renew our thinking to get to that place. As we freely receive from God, we're positioned to freely give to those whom God directs us to[13]. Like Abraham, our father in the faith, we are blessed to be a blessing[14].

"Tell those who are rich not to be proud and not to trust in their money, which will soon be gone, but their pride and trust should be in the living God who always richly gives us all we need for our enjoyment. Tell them to use their money to do good. They should be rich in good works and should give happily to those in need, always being ready to share with others whatever God has given them. By doing this they will be storing up real treasure for themselves in heaven—it is the only safe investment for eternity! And they will be living a fruitful Christian life down here as well."
(1 Timothy 6:17-19 (TLB))

It Needs to Start Now

One of the biggest mistakes we can make as Christians is to wait until we feel we have enough for ourselves before we commit to the financial principles God sets out in His Word.

It's a mistake because it demonstrates our faith is not in God as our Provider, but in how much we have. To move into the fullness of what God has planned for us, we need to start with what we've got. It's as we show ourselves faithful with the little, that we demonstrate we can be trusted with a lot[15]. In a way, we can't afford *not* to take advantage of the time when we only have a little, because it's the opportunity to demonstrate to God we're committed to His way of doing things. Trusting Him when we ourselves may be struggling financially is what gets God's attention, in the same way the widow got Jesus' attention when she gave all she had into the treasury[16].

As you read on through the book and start to understand God's ways of dealing with finances, don't put off applying the Biblical principles until a time where you feel you're in a better position to do so. Start now, because God's way of handling finances is the true hope we have to bring us out of debt. Debt can sometimes make us feel we're in a hole with no way of getting out. What God does however is offer us a 'rope' so we can get out of the hole we've fallen into. God's way of dealing with finances, which He sets out in His Word and is revealed to us by the Holy Spirit, is the 'rope' we're looking for. If we're willing to humble ourselves and ask for His help[17], trust what He says in His Word[18], it won't be long before we know we're on our way out of the hole.

1. Take time to make a list of five people, families, or organizations you would like to help financially. It may be simply buying someone a weekly food shop, helping someone pay off a debt, or a charity with a vision to alleviate poverty in the third world. Make a note below of who you have on your heart:

1.

2.

3.

4.

5.

2. Start praying about the list of people / organizations you have identified as those you would like to help. Ask God to bring you to the place financially where you're able to fulfil the desire of your heart to help those on your list. Pray about the list regularly, thanking God for placing these people and organizations on your heart.

Part 2

The Two Financial Systems

7

The Two Financial Systems

There are two main ways of dealing with finances - the world's way; and God's way. This second part of the book is aimed at bringing clarity regarding these two systems, not simply so we can understand the sharp contrast that exists between them, but also to help us get to a place where we can make an *informed choice* regarding which financial system we're going to commit to. If we're looking to God to help us become debt-free, we have to make a conscious decision to choose His system. Having a 'foot in both camps' is not an option for the Christian who wants to prosper, because as we'll see, the laws and principles governing these two systems are very different. We have to choose whether our allegiance lies with the world's way of doing things, or God's.

Poles Apart

The world's economic system, and God's economic system could not be further apart from each other in the way they operate. They are completely different in the laws that govern them; the purpose for their existence; the principles on which they are founded; as well as the fruit they produce. Over the next few chapters, we'll be unpacking these various elements a little more.

The stability of a building is dependent on the foundation it is built upon. If the foundation is weak or flawed in any way,

59

there is a danger that whatever is built on top of it will be subject to failure. Because the world economic system has been born out of the fallen nature of man, it is subject to collapse. That's why we see catastrophic economic events such as the Great Depression of 1929 and the financial crash of 2008, bringing with them the costly toll of mass unemployment and reduced incomes. It is man, out of a nature that became spoiled when sin entered at the Fall[1] that has birthed the world financial system. The prophet Jeremiah tells us *"A human heart is more dishonest than anything else. It can't be healed. Who can understand it?"*[2]. The apostle Paul reinforces this when he says *"I know that nothing good lives in me; that is, nothing good lives in my corrupt nature."*[3]. The world's economic system has been created out of the fallen nature of man, it is independent of God, and so it is subject to failure. Putting our trust in it is therefore foolish, especially once we realize there's a better financial system available to us - God's.

God's financial system on the other hand is perfect because He Himself has created it. He is righteous[4], and so the method He has set up for dealing with finances is righteous. It is not corrupt or flawed in any way. God didn't need to consult man when He created His system[5] because He already had the perfect wisdom that was needed[6]. Because there hasn't been any human involvement in setting up God's system, it's not affected by changes in the political or social climate. Whatever happens in the world around us does not affect God's financial system - it still works whether there is an abundance, or a famine in the world. The patriarch Isaac is an example of this, prospering even though there was a famine in the land[7]. God's system is not dependent on who holds political power, nor does it depend on which monetary system a particular country may be implementing. For the individual who chooses to operate within God's system, it is guaranteed to bring them success, because it is God Himself who has founded it[8].

Both Systems Reflect Their Founder

The world's financial system reflects the nature of the ones who created it - sinful man. Until a person is born-again of the Spirit of God through faith in Christ, they are a slave to the sinful nature[9]. It is this old unregenerate nature that causes people to be selfish, because they are bound by a hunger to indulge the selfish nature[10]. This leads people to seek, generate, and then accumulate more and more money in an attempt to gratify the flesh. I've experienced this personally, and if it hadn't been for the grace of God in my life it would have eventually led to my complete destruction[11].

The flesh is what causes the world system to be centered around *personal* profit and gain, which will always be at the expense of others - the poor. At the end of 2020, it was estimated nearly half of the world's global assets (43%) were owned by the richest 1% of the world's population. The 'ultra-rich' account for only 0.1% of the world population, yet they own 25% of the world's wealth. The bottom 50% of the world's population owned only 1% of global wealth between them[12]. It grieves the heart of God when the poor are exploited and ignored[13], which is why we're warned that *"A person who gets ahead by oppressing the poor or by showering gifts on the rich will end in poverty"*[14].

The world financial system is geared around selfish desire, whereas God's system is geared around helping others. In the same way the world system reflects the nature of the ones who created it, God's system reflects the nature of the One who created *it*. His economic system looks towards meeting *everybody's* need, not just the individual. The founder of this system is Himself a generous Giver, and so the system He has created cannot help but reflect His nature. God is looking to meet the needs of the individual who trusts in Him, and then provide them with an abundance so they in turn are able to meet the needs of others. This is simply an expression of who God is. For the Christian who commits to God's ways of doing things, not only will He give them the resources to be generous, He will also give them the heart to want to do it. A generous heart needs to come first however, because without His heart of generosity within us, it's impossible for us to be the generous stewards God has planned for us to be. If the whole church were to capture the generous heart of God, and then engage fully with His system, nobody would be left out.

Operating But Not Participating

It's important to point out that the Christian *does need* to operate within the world's financial system, but they don't have to engage with its unrighteous practices. Christians shouldn't be involved in practices such as cheating, lying, and stealing to make increase. A faith in Christ leads to the individual becoming born-again in their spirit, so they become a new person on the inside[15]. This new nature[16] which is born from above[17], is a reflection of the One who is both righteous and generous[18]. Therefore, as born-again believers in Christ we have the ability to operate righteously, as well as generously within a system where so many are operating unrighteously and selfishly. It's in the Christian's DNA to walk righteously once they are born-again[19].

Though followers of Christ are *in* the world, they are not *of* the world[20]. Though they operate *in* the world's financial system, they are not *of* the world's financial system. The Christian is called to manage their finances in line with different laws and principles to the world, principles which are set out for us in God's Word. We will be looking at God's system in more detail in Part 3 ("God's Financial System"), but only to say for now that if we ask God, He will give us His grace (His spiritual ability and strength) so that we can manage our finances in a way that honors Him - both righteously and generously[21].

Practical Exercise

Take some time to make a comprehensive list of all your **Regular _Fixed_ Payments.** Some may be weekly, the majority are likely to be monthly, but there may also be one or two that are annual. Go through all your bank and credit card accounts so that you don't miss any off your list. Make a note of the _amount_ you're paying, as well as _who you're paying it to._ Keep this list for later on in the book, but remember to add any new payments you may set up in the meantime.

8

Understanding the Battle

Unless we've grown up in a Christian family where we've been taught Biblical principles of money management, the only system we're familiar with is the world system. Because we know how the world system works, we're comfortable with it. The world's way of doing things has become our 'norm' to the extent that when we're introduced to God's way of dealing with finances, our minds are challenged by it. This is because God's way involves *faith*, which always challenges the natural mind because the mind relies on reasoning and understanding. As we begin to understand more about God's financial system, we must be prepared for the battle that will come between what our flesh wants to do (or not do as is often the case); and what the Spirit is leading us to do. The choice to follow the leading of the flesh, or the leading of the Spirit, is ours. However, God can only take us to His best if we follow the Spirit, which involves making choices that reflect our trust in Him as He takes us forward.

The way God thinks and the way natural man thinks are entirely different. In Isaiah 55:8-9, we read how God says: *"My thoughts are nothing like your thoughts,"* says the Lord. *"And my ways are far beyond anything you could imagine. For just as the heavens are higher than the earth, so my ways are higher than your ways and my thoughts higher than your thoughts"*[1]. These verses make it clear how there is a huge gap between how God thinks, and the way man (and woman) thinks. Natural man is not even close to being able to think like God. Figuratively speaking, not only is man on a different level to God, he's actually on a different planet!

Renewal of the Mind

This is the reason the Bible tells us we need to renew our minds. It's through having our minds *renewed* that we experience the fulness of what God has in store for us[2]. Renewal of the mind simply means we have to replace our old way of thinking, taught to us by the world, with God's way of thinking, taught to us from the Bible[3]. The challenge however is this; because there's such a big gap between the way God thinks and the way man thinks, some of the things God says do not make sense to us, so our flesh tries to resist them[4]. The natural mind cannot accept the things of God[5], which is why we need to believe God *by faith*. We need to make the choice to believe God because we trust Him, not because we've got evidence to support *why* we should trust Him.

The renewal of the mind doesn't involve simply 'tweaking' how we think. God is not looking for us to tidy things up around the edges, because the scriptures demand we undergo a *total* renewal in the way we think so we can catch up with God's way of thinking. That's a very big ask! As we renew our minds with God's Word however, it will naturally lead to us to *do* the things God does, thereby reflecting His goodness here on earth[6].

It's a great relief to realize we've not been left to our own devices to try to figure out how to renew our minds so we can get to God's standard of thinking. The beauty of the Gospel is that through the born-again experience we're given 'the mind of Christ'[7]. It's a gift that comes to us at salvation[8]. Our responsibility is to then surrender to the Holy Spirit and work with Him towards the renewal of our mind. This renewal, the complete regeneration in the way we think, will lead to 'the mind of Christ' becoming our dominant way of thinking so we can catch up with God's way of thinking, which includes the area of finances.

God has given us all we need to win the battle to renew our minds because He's given us the Holy Spirit. The Holy Spirit is the only One who knows what God's thoughts are, and He is willing to share them with us![9] If we're prepared to humble ourselves to be taught and counselled by Him, the process of having our minds renewed knows no limits[10].

Walking on Water

Peter, a follower of Jesus, experienced first-hand the fight to renew his mind so he could think, and then do the things God does. He was in a boat with the other disciples when a fierce storm started to thrash the vessel. Jesus then came alongside, walking on the water. Once the disciples recognized Jesus and calmed themselves down, Peter asked for permission to walk towards Jesus on the water. Jesus said to him 'Come!', so Peter got out of the boat and started walking on the water. We know Peter was doing this *by faith*, because once his natural mind kicked in and he realized how contrary the conditions were, he began to sink. The reason he didn't drown was because Jesus rescued him[11].

I love this account of Peter for a number of reasons. In the midst of the storm, even with the boat being battered from every direction by the wind and waves, staying in the boat was the safest place for the disciples to be. Yet Peter, once he'd heard Jesus say 'Come!' *stepped out by faith*, and did what seemed impossible - he walked on water in the middle of the storm. His flesh (his natural mind) must have been yelling at him at the top of its voice to stop being so stupid. But because he'd heard Jesus say "Come", it overruled every other voice that was trying to stop him. Even though it was brief, by walking on the water Peter saw the impossible become a reality for him.

Step Out of the Boat

By inviting us to commit how we deal with money to His way of doing things, God is inviting us to step out of the boat. We may not be in a literal storm, but the debt we have may be making us feel like we're drowning. Jesus is saying to us, like He did to Peter, "Come!". He's saying to us to get out of our boat - to be prepared to step out of the ways we've done things in the past, ways we're familiar and comfortable with, and to start doing things His way. The danger we all face as followers of Christ is to refuse to step out of the boat when we hear God calling us. The circumstances around us, as well as our natural reasoning and logic, will try to stop us taking the step of faith God is asking us to take. We then end up staying in the boat because it's where we feel safe. We *wish* we could do what we see others doing, we *wish* we could get out of debt, but we're not willing to take the steps that are needed to see the impossible become a reality in our lives.

God is inviting each one of us to step out of our boat and to trust Him with our finances. As we come into a clearer understanding of His thoughts, together with His encouragement to embrace His ways of doing things, we need to be prepared for the flesh to rebel, because the flesh won't like it. *The flesh will try to oppose where God wants to take us by faith.*

In the next three chapters we will continue to look at how vastly different God's way of thinking is to man's thinking in the area of finance. In getting a clearer understanding of the contrast between man and God's thoughts in this area, we're better prepared for the resistance that will come against us from the flesh[12]. That way, we're in a stronger position to bring the flesh into submission[13]. My prayer as we close this chapter is that each one of us will humble ourselves before God, ask the Holy Spirit to teach us God's way of thinking, and then give us the faith and courage we need to start managing our finances in the way He has prescribed for us.

Practical Exercise

Make a comprehensive list of where the majority of your money is spent over a typical month, but don't include the *Regular Fixed Payment'* list you made at the end of the last chapter. Include things like gasoline, how much you spend on food (supermarket / eating out / takeaway etc.); hairdresser, pocket money for the kids etc. Try to capture as many areas of expenditure as you can for a typical month, so it may take you time to bring the whole list together, adding things as you remember them. Keep this *'General Spending List'* until further on in the book.

9

Hoarders and Givers

The aim of the next three chapters is to highlight particular areas where the contrast between the world's view of finances, and God's view of finances can be seen clearly. Understanding some of the key differences between the two systems brings an appreciation of how unique God's approach to finances is. It also helps bring the 'mind shift'[1] that's required for those who choose God's system, so they can be in step with how God wants them to deal with money.

One way to appreciate the contrast is to look at how an individual responds when they're having difficulty making ends meet. When things are a bit tight financially, people usually start to rein things in and try to become more disciplined in their spending. Depending on their situation, they may also look to borrow money from somewhere - from friends or relatives; from the bank; or put payments on credit cards. The other area they will look at is their charitable giving, and it's likely they'll stop giving money to the organizations they may be supporting. The world's attitude is 'charity begins at home', so making these adjustments is the way most people will try to manage lean times. From a natural, human perspective these are reasonable steps to take, and nobody should be judged for taking these actions.

When we come over to God's system however, there is a better way of doing things when it gets a bit tight financially. We still need to be responsible with stewarding what we have, but the Bible teaches us that even when we ourselves are experiencing lean times, we need to continue to be generous towards others. There may be a need to *adjust* what we give to ensure we're giving within our means[2], but stopping our giving completely is not a Biblical recommendation.

Being Generous

Jesus said *"Give, and you will receive. Your gift will return to you in full—pressed down, shaken together to make room for more, running over, and poured into your lap. The amount you give will determine the amount you get back"*[3]. If we choose to show kindness towards people, others will show kindness towards us, but in a greater measure. If we choose to be judgmental towards people, we will be judged to a greater degree than we judged others. If we choose to be generous towards others with our money, we will also see more come back to us. As we give however, it's important to make sure we're giving for the right reasons, motivated by a compassion and generosity to help others, not because we understand the spiritual principle and are tempted to give for selfish gain. As we show generosity in our giving, motivated by mercy and compassion, we will be reflecting the heart of God to those around us[4].

Solomon tells us: *"It is possible to give away and become richer! It is also possible to hold on too tightly and lose everything. Yes, the liberal man shall be rich! By watering others, he waters himself"*[5]. Being generous is an expression of God's heart - it's something that's natural to Him. We're meant to reflect His heart by being generous to others, and as we do, God's generosity will come back to us in a greater measure. This is God's way of doing things. It is a spiritual principle that governs every part of our lives, including money.

Hearing God say in His Word the way to increase is to keep being generous is extremely challenging to the natural mind. The natural mind is so used to doing things in completely the opposite way that it will try to resist the truth of what God is saying - it cannot see the sense in how parting with money will bring increase. It will shout at us in the same way it shouted at Peter not to be so stupid in stepping out of the boat when there was a storm raging around him. Nonetheless, it is what God says in His Word - if we give, it will come back to us in greater measure.

Nobody can be, or should be *persuaded* to believe what God says is true, because each and every person has to take the step of faith to trust God for *themselves*. The disciples who stayed in the boat weren't the ones to convince Peter he needed to step out of the boat - he himself made the choice to trust Jesus when he heard the command "Come"![6] Having decided to trust and take the step of faith, it was only Peter that experienced the supernatural. None of the other disciples did because they stayed in the boat. God has created every individual with free-will, He has given us a personal freedom to choose whether to believe Him or not. It is the choices an individual makes regarding what God says in His Word that determines whether they experience natural, or supernatural results.

Choose Faith

We've already touched on how *faith* is a key ingredient in God's financial system, which is why we have to take a *different* attitude to what is regarded as 'normal' (the world's way of doing things). The individual who wants to see their debts cleared *supernaturally* in God's financial system cannot afford to operate the world's way - they have to operate *by faith* in God's Word. Faith is the supernatural tool God has given to every believer[7], so they can see the supernatural results they desire when they apply it.

Faith is simply choosing to believe what God says in His Word, then acting on what He's says[8]. When we're willing to do that, we're actually expressing our trust in His nature and character. We're making the statement we believe He is faithful to the promises He has given, even though we have no physical evidence to support what we believe. Because giving to see increase is totally foreign to the natural mind, we need to *trust the Lord with all our HEART, and not lean on our own understanding* in making the decision to do what He says[9]. That's when we'll be like Peter, taking a step of faith in the absence of being able to understand with the natural mind how it works. Let's not be the ones who stay in the boat, looking at others who are experiencing God's help to get out of debt. Let's be the ones who are walking on water, choosing to take the steps of faith God is inviting us to take.

As we look to God to be set free from the burden of financial debt, we need to make the decision to be a giver, not a hoarder. Making a decision to be generous is an extremely powerful statement, especially when we ourselves are in a time of lack.

Being generous to others when we're looking to clear our own debt is the opportunity to show God we really trust Him with our finances, and are committed to His ways. The natural mind will try to tell us we're crazy, but because we've heard His voice, we're willing to step out of the boat and trust Him. As we choose to do things God's way, we're effectively putting our signature on a *'Declaration of Allegiance'* - we're boldly stating that our future is in God's system of dealing with finances, not the world's.

Make a list of all the credit card debts you owe, as well as any other outstanding loans you may have that are not yet paid off (excluding your mortgage at this stage). Make a note of the interest rate you are being charged for each one. List them in descending order of interest (highest interest rate at the top), and keep this *'Credit Card & Loan List'* until later in the book.

10

Dealing with Others

The second area of contrast between God's way of dealing with money, and the world's way of dealing with money can be seen when we look at how individuals *deal with each other* within each of the separate systems. When left to his own devices, natural man is willing to use immoral and corrupt practices towards others in an attempt to gain more money. God's system however, without exception, employs righteous practices on the journey to seeing increase.

The Soft Toy Story

Many years ago before I became a Christian, Jill and I went into a local, family-owned furniture shop to look for a new bed. We had an above average income at the time, so it wasn't a struggle for us to buy the bed we wanted. After deciding on a bed, I then started to haggle with the shop owner in an attempt to get the price down. He was very pleasant about it and agreed to a reduction. Wanting the bed for the lowest possible price, I wasn't satisfied, so I continued to haggle the price down. It was when I realized the shopkeeper thought I was trying to get a reduction because we couldn't afford the bed, that I started to feel uncomfortable about the situation. In an attempt to help me, he offered to reduce it further if we weren't paying by credit card because that would reduce his overheads. He also offered for us to delay paying until our next paycheck if that would help us. I felt so awkward and embarrassed at this stage that all I wanted to do was close the deal and get out of the shop as quickly as I could!

As we were making our way out through the shop however, the shopkeeper gave our two-year-old daughter a display toy just before we got to the door. In my embarrassment I was nearly pleading with him at this stage not to, but to no avail. He was insistent, I suspect he wanted to make sure the little girl had at least one toy to play with! As we headed back to the car, I could tell Jill wasn't impressed with what I had just done. The cold silence between us was only broken by the delight of our little girl thrilled with her new toy!

That incident has stayed with me even though it is now well over thirty years since it happened. Thankfully, I've learnt some lessons from it. I came to recognize my insistence in haggling over the price was because I was greedy. I was driven by a selfish desire to want more, even though we already had a lot. I've also come to see how I showed a total lack of respect for the shop owner, being indifferent to the fact he needed to make a profit to feed his family and keep his business viable. Nowadays, I'm still happy to negotiate a good deal, but it's always with respect for the other party so that both sides come out of it with a fair deal, not just me. That's one of the ways the grace of God has made a difference in my life.

A Wider Problem

The attitude of heart I displayed that day is not uncommon. Though many will not end up in the embarrassing situation I did, the approach of trying to haggle a price down as much as possible with little or no regard for the person they are dealing with is widespread. Unfortunately, it's the world's way of doing things.

Another trait of a system that is out to meet the individual's needs as a first priority is cheating the taxman. People will work 'cash-in-hand' so there's no proof of a transaction if any questions are raised. Yet another common practice is to stay silent when undercharged for something, or when they're given too much change at the till. They keep silent thinking it's a 'blessing', which it's not because they are gaining at someone else's expense. It is important to point out not everybody operates this way, but these practices are so prevalent they are regarded as the 'norm'. Those who point out to a shopkeeper when they've been undercharged, or when they've been given too much change at the till are usually thanked for their honesty. What a sad reflection on a system that feels it needs to congratulate honesty when it presents itself.

The Contrast

Stepping over into God's financial system is like stepping onto a different planet - the contrast is so sharp. The principles God sets out include making sure we deal fairly and honestly with other people in every area of our lives, including the area of finances. When the Bible tells us we need to use 'honest scales', it is referring to making sure we don't short-change anybody along the way[1]. God hates it when people are dishonest in their dealings[2], and gives a sobering warning that He will deal with those who are involved in such practices[3].

When we pay our taxes, we are expected to act righteously, which means paying the correct amount, and on time. Some Pharisees tried to trick Jesus by asking Him whether it was right to pay taxes to those who they regarded as their enemies - the Romans. Jesus took a coin, and pointing to Caesar's image He replied *"Give to Caesar what belongs to Caesar and give to God what belongs to God"*[4]. We may resent the taxman for taking money from us, seeing him as an enemy, when all he (or she) is doing is what they have been appointed to do. The apostle Paul makes the point very clearly when he says: *"Every person must obey the rulers over him. Every ruler has his power from God. And the rulers are put there by God. So anyone who fights against the ruler, fights against what God put there. And those who fight will be punished. The rulers do not bring fear to a good man, but they bring fear to a bad man. If you do not want to be afraid of a ruler, do what is good and he will praise you"*[5]. The fruit of operating the world's way is a lack of peace, whereas doing things God's way brings the peace we've been created to enjoy. Peace allows us to sleep at night, knowing we've acted with integrity in paying what we owe, in line with a heart that loves God[6].

God's system also involves paying what something is worth, not necessarily what we can get it for. Even if we can get the price down by haggling as I did, if it's worth more, then we should pay the higher price. This is a lesson I learned from reading about Abraham's life. Following the death of his wife Sarah, Abraham wanted to buy a burial plot for his family. Even though he was a foreigner in the land, Abraham was so highly respected by those who lived around him that the landowner offered to give him the burial ground free of charge. Abraham insisted on paying the asking price for the land however[7]. Having walked with God for decades Abraham understood the heart of God. It's out of this relationship with God that Abraham acted with integrity, insisting he paid the correct price out of respect for the person he was dealing with.

King David was the same. He was a man with a heart after God[8], and again we read how he insisted on paying for the threshing floor he'd asked for. Even though he was offered the plot for free, along with the sacrifice to go on it, he insisted on paying[9].

Of course, there are occasions when it's right to accept things as a gift from other people. We need to learn how to recognize the times when God is blessing us through others, and give Him glory for it. But in the area of business in particular, and that includes shopping at the local store, it's important to consider the other party's interest as well, not just our own.

"In whatever you do, don't let selfishness or pride be your guide. Be humble, and honor others more than yourselves"[10]. In a world where so much is centered on self-gain, we need to adopt God's heart and look beyond our own selfish desires, so that we can more accurately reflect Him to the world around us.

Understanding the Contrast

The reason people cheat, lie, and steal, putting themselves at the center with no regard for others is because every person has inherited a corrupt, fallen nature as a result of the Fall[11]. When God created Adam, He breathed spiritual life into him[12], and in that life was the faith Adam needed to look to God for his provision. God had already provided everything Adam needed before He created him[13], so all Adam needed to do was trust God.

Mankind became separated from God at the Fall because of Adam's disobedience, with the result that his faith in God as his Provider was lost. Adam now found himself in the position of needing to look to *himself* for his provision, and out of his fallen, corrupt nature became inward-focused, which we know as selfishness. Rather than looking *outward* to God for provision, humanity now has to look *inward* to themselves for survival, all as a result of the Fall. With an attitude of 'the survival of the fittest', man doesn't care what practices he needs to engage in to survive, or who gets damaged in the process.

The only way to remedy this tragic situation is by becoming born-again, which comes through faith in Christ[14]. This is when the Spirit of God comes into a person's heart, and with this restoration comes the faith to see God as their Provider - the very faith that was lost at the Fall. The new creation[15], born from above[16], is once more capable of looking *outward* to God for their provision. As a child of God, they now look to their Father for their provision, and as confidence grows in His goodness and ability to provide, they realize they don't need to employ the corrupt practices of the world to have their needs met. They simply need to trust God, and put their faith in His faithfulness as a Father[17]. Their source will never run dry, because He is *Yehôvâh Yir'eh - "The LORD Will Provide"*[18].

None of us are in a position to judge the world system, nor to judge those who operate in its wrong practices. This is because all of us, at one stage or another have come from the place of being under the dominion of the sinful nature, and so have been prone to its practices. We've all done things we now know to be wrong, including this area of how we've dealt with others financially. If it weren't for God's saving grace, we'd still be operating in those unrighteous ways, because it's what was natural to us before we were introduced to God's righteousness (His way of doing things)[19]. It is only when a person experiences the grace of God, and with it the gift of righteousness[20], that they can start to walk a new path[21]. That's when they become 'salt and light' in the world[22], demonstrating a healthy, righteous way of dealing with finances.

Breaking Free

Hopefully, the stark contrast between how the world deals with money, and God's way of dealing with money is becoming increasingly clear to us. With this clarity comes the challenge of deciding which system we're going to commit to. Whatever system we choose, our commitment needs to be total. We can't have a foot in both camps, it simply doesn't work that way. Committing to God's system means we're choosing to swim against the tide, it will involve making decisions that show integrity, based on God's righteousness. There is a cost to walking righteously with finances[23], but there is also a cost to *not* walking righteously. When we're not prepared to follow God's way, we're effectively allowing the tide of the world system to take us wherever it wants to.

Let's be a people who make choices that cause us to stand out from the crowd for the right reasons - choices where we're seen as people who are honest, truthful, and reliable. Let's honor people when we deal with them, not just financially but in every area of our lives. When people ask us why we're different, we can point to the One who has given us the grace to be different.

Unlike the world that measures prosperity by how much money an individual has, true prosperity from a heavenly perspective includes peace, joy, and righteousness, as well as an abundance to help others[24]. The peace that comes from knowing we've acted with integrity and righteousness makes us happy. It is this peace that settles our soul, allowing us to sleep at night knowing we're doing what God is asking us to do. Peace is a treasure we can't buy. Mind you, there's no need to, because it's already been bought for us by Jesus[25]. All we need to do is walk in His ways and His peace will find us[26].

Unfortunately, the spending habits we develop over the years can hold us back from the fullness of what God has for us. Take some time over the next few days to ask God to show you:

1. Any *items* you enjoy spending money on that are damaging you financially, and even emotionally. Are you drawn to buying specific items such as clothes, shoes, or tech gadgets (as examples) on a frequent basis, only feeling satisfied when you've acquired them? Ask God to reveal any items that have a hold on you, as well as to help you break free from the grip they have.

2. Any *people* in your life who are making it easy for you to be undisciplined in your spending. Do you need God's help to distance yourself from them, or to give you courage to say 'no' when you know it's wrong to spend time with them?

3. Any *routines* you need to change. An example would be going shopping every week because you feel the need to 'escape'; but you come back having spent money you don't have; on things you don't need. Again, ask God to reveal any specific areas to you. Ask Him also to help you break these habits, and to show you another activity you could do that will be healthier for your wallet (or purse), as well as healthier to your body, mind, and emotions.

11

Working to Give, Or to Get?

If you were asked the question *"Why do you go to work?"*; what would be your answer? I suspect the majority of people would say things like *"So I can pay my bills"*; *"So I can afford a nice vacation"*; *"To pay for my children's education"*; or *"So I can buy a nice car"*. That's the way I would have answered the question if I had been asked 30 years ago. However, because God has been working on me for quite some time now, I've come to understand there is a greater purpose to working than simply having our own needs met.

There is nothing wrong with working to pay the bills, to be able to afford a nice holiday, nor to be able to buy a new house or car. These things are good, but it's important we don't miss the broader purpose of why we work, which is revealed to us from the Word of God. In this chapter we'll explore a Biblical principle regarding work and see how it contrasts sharply with how the world thinks.

Challenged by The Truth

When I first came across Ephesians 4:28, my brain couldn't comprehend it. My mind had been so conditioned to thinking the only reason for working was to meet my own needs, I just couldn't understand why the apostle Paul said what he said. It was as if there was a thick, armored wall trying to stop the truth of what Paul was saying from penetrating. Having been trained by the world system to think so strongly in a particular way, when my mind encountered a truth it couldn't comprehend, it tried everything it could to resist it. My flesh was more than happy to keep *me* as the center of attention, but when the Spirit of God whispered there was more to working than having my own needs met, the 'sleeping giant' of the natural man was aroused and began to fight the truth I was hearing from the Word of God.

Writing to the followers of Christ in Ephesus, Paul said *"The one who steals must no longer steal; but rather he must labor, producing with his own hands what is good, **so that** he will have something to share with the one who has need"*[1]. As followers of Christ, hopefully the call to stop stealing is not too challenging for us. If it is, then we need to bring it to God so He can reform us. It's the second part of the verse that drew my attention, because it is here we read how the apostle Paul says we should work *"… **so that** (for the purpose of) having something to share with the one who has need"*. In other words, Paul is saying there is another motivation for working other than meeting our own needs, and that reason is so we can help meet the needs of others who are struggling. I had got so used to working to provide only for my own family and meet my own needs, that the concept of working to help other people refused to register with me for quite some time.

The world system we've grown up with has trained the natural man to think working is all about us - it's all about meeting our own needs, and no one else's. It takes the attitude *"I've earned it, so it's mine"*. That's the mindset I came from, which is why Paul's statement exhorting us to work *so that we can help others* was such a challenge to my thinking and understanding. But that's the way God thinks!

The Correct Perspective

We need to get this statement of Paul's into its proper perspective. Paul is not saying we should work *solely* for the purpose of helping other people, but he *is* saying it is something that needs to be on the list of *why* we work to earn money. We do need to go to work so we're able to pay our bills and look after our family. In fact, it's a Biblical mandate that as followers of Christ we make sure we care for and provide for our families[2]. Working so we can buy a new house, a new car, or have vacations is also a good thing because it is the 'reward' for the work of our hands. God wants us to enjoy these things in the same way earthly parents want to see their children enjoy things.

God's concern for His children is not so much what stuff they have; but whether the stuff has them! If the focus and motivation of our lives is centered on getting the next house, the next new car, or the next exotic holiday, then those things 'have' us and we're in danger of missing the true purpose of our existence. The primary purpose of why we exist is to enjoy God, to allow God to enjoy us, as well as to bring Him glory through the way we live our lives out of our relationship with Him as our Father.

Imitate God[3]

God is a Giver, and is continually looking for opportunities to *bless* people, not to take from them. It is this same mindset of giving He is asking His children to take on board, so that people who are looking at us will see what our Father is like[4]. God is looking for a people who are willing to trust Him, a people who will allow Him to put His heart within them[5], so they can accurately reflect His giving heart to the world around them.

Because of the way our minds have been shaped by the world system, the likelihood is when we look to God for His provision, we'll usually only ask for what we need. We'll ask Him to help us pay the unexpected bill, or provide the car we need. This is not a bad thing, because the fact we're looking to Him for His provision is a positive act of trust and faith. But when we ask, God wants us to go further - He doesn't want us to *only* ask for our own needs to be met, He wants us to be bold and ask for more than we need, so we can help others who are struggling.

Whether it's in our working or in our asking, the Kingdom of God approach is to look *beyond* having only our needs met, to a place where we have an excess to support others. That particular characteristic of our Father is already in our DNA from the time we're born of the Holy Spirit through receiving Christ. The Christian journey from then on is simply releasing the nature of Christ who has come to dwell in us so the world can see Him, working through us. As we pray for 'more than enough' in order to help others, even if the excess we have is only small to start with, it will still be helpful to someone. It will also help us, because giving even small amounts with a right heart helps us develop the giving mentality that more accurately reflects who our Father is. Giving to help others out of the little we have is also a statement to God that He can trust us with more.

Living as a Citizen

When we first come into the Kingdom of God, working so we can give some of it away to bring comfort to others is a totally foreign concept - it's simply not how the natural man works. The natural man's attention is always centered on himself - his needs first, then as a second priority, he'll look to meet even more of his own needs. Natural man likes to spend extravagantly on himself (or herself), even though some of the things he (or she) is buying may never see the light of day until it's time to take them to a thrift store.

A 'Kingdom of God mindset' displaces the individual from the center, and invites God to take His place on the throne of their hearts. When we're willing to do this, God brings *other people's needs* into our personal financial world, which prevents us from remaining self-focused. As He brings other people's needs to our attention, He is willing to finance what He's asking us to do, out of His own resources. As we continue to be faithful in generosity, the old selfish mindset that was trained so thoroughly by the world's system will slowly, and gradually be replaced by God's heart to give. Over time, God will change the desires of our hearts from a place of wanting more stuff for 'us', to a place where we want more stuff so we can give and help others. That's where Jesus' statement *'it is more blessed to give than to receive'*[6] changes from being words on a page, to becoming a true experience and reality.

The Ability to Choose

God has created every single person with the ability to choose what they believe. No matter how dark things seem, no matter what other freedoms may have been stripped away from them, the ability to choose what we believe can never be taken away from us. 'Fate' and 'luck' are not what determine our destiny - our destiny is governed by the choices we make. God does not choose to bless some people more than others[7]; those who display the favor of God on their lives are blessed because they have made *the choice* to believe what He says, and have walked with Him into the blessing He has promised. Worthiness or unworthiness doesn't come into God's equation either, it's all down to choosing whether we believe God, or not.

The grace of God is still being offered freely to *all* men (and women)[8], and it is those who <u>choose</u> to receive this freely-offered grace that receive it. It's in our choices that we choose life, or we choose death[9]. It's in our choices that we also make the spiritual declaration of who we trust[10]. If we choose God's way of dealing with finances by being obedient to His Word, then we're making the unspoken declaration that we trust Him. *In choosing His ways, we're also choosing the fruit that comes from doing things His way.* Faith in God's system brings rewards[11], but before the reward has to come the choice to believe.

What will you choose? Will you continue to trust a failing world system that only has the individual at the center? Or will you choose to trust God's system, a way of doing things that not only blesses the individual, but also gives the individual 'more than enough' so they can bless others as well? I pray you will choose life - the life that God is offering you.

> *"You can make this choice by loving the Lord your God, obeying him, and committing yourself firmly to him. This is the key to your life."*
>
> Deuteronomy 30:20 (NLT)

Practical Exercise

Deuteronomy 30:19-20a (NLT) says: *"Today I have given you the choice between life and death, between blessings and curses. Now I call on heaven and earth to witness the choice you make. Oh, that you would choose life, so that you and your descendants might live! You can make this choice by loving the Lord your God, obeying him, and committing yourself firmly to him. This is the key to your life."*

Take time with God to reflect on which financial system you are going to trust - the world's, or His. If you're able to come to the place where you are willing to trust God with your money, what does *"loving the Lord your God, obeying him, and committing yourself firmly to him"* with your finances look like to you at this stage of your journey? Make a note of some of the steps, and possibly the changes you need to make that reflect the commitment you're making.

1.

2.

3.

4.

5.

Part 3

God's Financial System

12

Keeping the Main Thing, the Main Thing

Committing our finances to God means we're pledging ourselves to doing things His way[1]. It's essential therefore we understand *how* His financial system works. There is little benefit in simply 'trying our best', hoping one day we'll see the result we desire, because that approach leads to frustration, disappointment, and even defeat. *Understanding* how God wants us to deal with money equips us with the tools we need to move forward towards our goal of debt-freedom. This next part of the book is written for the purpose of clarifying the various elements involved in God's financial system. This in turn will give us the confidence of knowing we're doing things His way, and so are heading in the direction He is taking us - towards debt-freedom.

Baking Bread

I like to bake bread. It won't surprise anybody that one thing I've learned over the years is how important the *ingredients* are. If I leave out an ingredient, or substitute an ingredient for something different, then the loaf doesn't turn out as planned. It's the same with God's financial system - if we leave out any of the key 'ingredients', there's a danger things won't turn out for us in the way we'd hoped. The chapters that follow are written to help us understand what some of those key ingredients are.

Baking bread doesn't end with simply knowing what the ingredients are. To make a successful loaf, *I need to do something* with those ingredients. There's a *practical side* to making bread, which involves kneading the dough, allowing it to prove a couple of times, then baking it in the oven. I have to *put into practice* the knowledge I have if I'm going to bake a loaf that can be eaten.

It's the same with God's financial system. It's not simply a case of *knowing* what's involved, we also have to *apply* the principles God is teaching us from His Word. It's important to get the knowledge in the first instance, but then the additional step of putting the knowledge into practice is equally important in order to see the desired result. Faith <u>and</u> works are required[2]. The faith part is coming into the understanding of what God's Word teaches us about finances, and then choosing to believe what He says. The works part is the practical application - actually *doing* what God is teaching us from His Word. This may sound easy in practice, but as we've read previously, the challenge comes when the flesh tries everything it can to hold us back. When we know God is asking us to take a step forward, and we choose to do it in obedience, these are the times we grow in faith in our Christian walk with God.

There's an element to the baking process that remains a mystery to me - I don't understand what happens to the ingredients as they come together to make a loaf. It's the same with God's financial system, how the various elements come together to bake the 'loaf' of debt-freedom is a mystery. That's because the *supernatural* part is God's part, not ours. As long as we do our part, as revealed to us by God in His Word, then add faith into the mix (believing things will turn out as God promises), we don't need to worry ourselves with the part we don't understand.

The Journey

You've heard me say how becoming debt-free is a *journey*, not a one-time event. There is a moment in time when we celebrate paying our last creditor, but before we get to that moment, we have a journey to travel. *The journey is more important than the event, because the journey is the opportunity we're presented with to grow in our relationship with God as our Father.* If we make it our priority to seek a deeper knowledge and revelation of His heart as we journey towards financial freedom, not only will we be debt-free when the time comes, but we'll also have a stronger relationship with God. It's a deeper, stronger relationship with God that brings the true, lasting peace we're looking for, not the debt-freedom.

It's out of our *relationship* with Him that He shares His wisdom and His righteousness with us[3]. It's because of our *relationship* with Him we grow to trust Him more and more, and will experience His faithfulness in meeting all our needs[4]. It's as we grow in our *relationship* with Him we learn to take steps of faith, building up our spiritual muscles. It's out of *relationship* He reveals His love for us as a Father, and so our love for Him grows. It's because of our *relationship* that God imparts His very own heart within us, so His priorities become ours[5]. If we make our *relationship* with Him the main thing as we journey towards debt-freedom[6], learning to trust and apply what He's teaching us, we'll be drawing closer to Him, as well as to our destination of being free from debt[7]. Debt-freedom is one of the unavoidable consequences of drawing closer to God, in the same way that getting wet is an unavoidable consequence of jumping into water.

We can see our goal of financial freedom on the horizon, and we're walking towards it, but let's take full advantage of the journey by growing closer to Him, and seeking His heart as our life's priority. On our journey, let's allow Him to teach us His ways, giving Him a freedom to impart His wisdom onto us. Let's seize the opportunity to grow to trust Him fully, because as we do that, it becomes easier to take the steps of faith that are necessary to see success.

Practical Exercise

1. Spend some time checking your motivation as to why you want to become debt-free. Ask yourself the question and write your reasons below. Bring them before God, and ask Him to tell you whether these are healthy reasons, (righteous), or not. Ask Him to help you weed out any that are unhealthy.

2. Pray and ask God to give you a heart that keeps Him at the center of your journey towards debt-freedom, so that when you reach your destination, the relationship you have with Him will be stronger than ever

13

Faith for Acceleration

Jesus was at a wedding in Cana in Galilee, when a crisis arose - the wine ran out. This would have been an extremely embarrassing situation for the hosts. Jesus saved the day however, because it was at this wedding that He performed His first miracle by turning water into wine. Jesus went 'above and beyond' what was needed, because not only was the shortage of wine addressed, He also provided the best wine of the day[1].

By turning the water into wine, Jesus defied all the natural laws governing wine-making. Even as someone who doesn't know a lot about wine-making, I know enough to understand there is a natural process that cannot be rushed. The grapes need time to grow, to be harvested, and then pressed. They are then added as the key ingredient to start the fermentation process. To make a good quality wine similar to the one Jesus provided, there also needs to be an aging process.

Jesus didn't produce the wine for this wedding by going through the natural process, He provided it *supernaturally*. Turning the water into wine was a miracle. A miracle is a process or event that is outside the boundaries of natural and scientific laws. Unfortunately, many people dismiss miracles because they're not willing to accept there's anything beyond what they can explain or understand with their natural intellect. They will try to explain them away by saying they are coincidences, or a deception, in the same way a magician deceives. The person who experiences a genuine miracle however is in no doubt they exist, because the transforming power of a miracle changes a life to the extent that the supernatural intervention of God cannot be denied.

Those who do not accept the reality of miracles are losing out on so much, because sadly they are limiting themselves to the boundaries of their own natural understanding and experience. Their highest authority is themselves - they take the view that if they cannot understand or give an explanation for something, then it must not be true. That's what it means to be carnal - only believing something is real and true if they can understand it through their own intellect, or discern it through their senses.

Faith for Acceleration

There are other examples in Jesus' ministry where there was an acceleration of the natural process of events. The disciples were in a boat with Jesus when a fierce storm rose up. It was so violent, they feared for their lives despite some of them being experienced fishermen[2]. Given time, the storm would have eventually subsided and the sea would have become calm again. The problem was that waiting for the storm to pass naturally would have cost lives, because the boat was already filling up with water and so the disciples would likely have drowned. Time wasn't on their side as far as this storm was concerned. Jesus intervened and used His faith to rebuke the storm and it stopped. What would have eventually come to a natural conclusion was accelerated by Jesus using His faith.

Cursing a fig tree and causing it to shrivel from the roots up is another example of Jesus accelerating a natural process[3]. What would have taken decades to happen naturally, started immediately once Jesus had cursed it. Again, Jesus was able to accelerate the natural, scientific process because of His faith.

There are also examples in the Old Testament of how God can accelerate a process supernaturally. One of these is when Nehemiah faced the almost impossible task of rebuilding the walls of Jerusalem. Together with those who had a passion for the project, the task was completed in only fifty-two days. Even his enemies were surprised, admitting how God must have played a part in this miracle[4].

God made a promise to His people that He would accelerate the natural processes of science and nature. Through the prophet Amos, God said *"the plowman will overtake the reaper"*[5]. That means the one who is plowing the field in preparation for sowing, will be doing so even before the previous harvest has been brought in. The natural mind cannot explain how a field can be prepared for sowing when there's already a crop on it waiting to be harvested. That's why it's supernatural! The Message translation of the same verse says *"things are going to happen so fast your head will swim, one thing fast on the heels of the other. You won't be able to keep up. Everything will be happening at once—and everywhere you look, blessings!"*[6]

God is the One who created science and nature, but He didn't do it in such a way that He would be limited by what He had created. God has the ability to act *beyond* the boundaries of His own creation, which is why we use the term supernatural (above the natural). This is the reason He could make a promise to accelerate things through the prophet Amos; why He was able to help Nehemiah reach his goal far quicker; as well as demonstrate His supernatural power through His Son Jesus.

No matter how impossible a debt may appear in the natural therefore, there's no reason He won't do the same today for those who put their faith in Him to help them get free[7].

Faith for the Supernatural

It's possible for a financial debt to be cleared by *natural* means. This involves being faithful with regular repayments, (probably over a number of years), good discipline, as well as self-control. In themselves these things are good, but the *natural* process of becoming debt-free is not where the emphasis of this book lies. Without neglecting those necessary disciplines, this book is written with the purpose of introducing *faith* into the equation, so that the reliance is not on the natural process, but rather a faith that God will intervene *supernaturally* to deliver the individual from the bondage of debt. *As a result of faith,* God is able to add something supernatural to our situation, something we're not able to do for ourselves.

When we believe God's promise to bring us into a place of financial freedom, and then follow His guidance as we journey towards our goal[8], we're giving God *permission* to intervene supernaturally on our behalf. God wants to help us, and our faith is the green light He needs to become involved so we can see our dream become a reality. My hope is that individuals, as well as couples, will be encouraged to believe God to *accelerate* the process by which their debts are removed. The result will be people reaching their goal a lot quicker; being able to experience debt-freedom much earlier; and therefore enjoy the benefits that financial freedom brings for a longer period of time.

God Responds to Faith

"It's impossible to please God apart from faith. And why? Because anyone who wants to approach God must believe both that he exists and that he cares enough to respond to those who seek him".

(Hebrews 11:6 (MSG).

God does not respond to *need*, nor does He respond to *desire* - God responds to faith. If God responded to need, His wealth of resources would have already met every need there is in the world. Similarly, if God responded to desire, all of our desires would already have been met. God is a loving Father who wants to meet our needs and desires[9], but without faith He's not able to do so. Faith is the currency whereby we receive our needs and desires from God[10].

Faith is the foundation of God's system, whether it be a financial need or anything else we're seeking from Him. Until we add faith into the mix of what we're believing for we'll remain frustrated. Hebrews 4:2 tells us: *"For this wonderful news—the message that God wants to save us—has been given to us just as it was to those who lived in the time of Moses. But it didn't do them any good because they didn't believe it. They didn't mix it with faith"*[11]. Let's not be like the Israelites of old, who even though they heard the promises of God, didn't experience the fulfilment because they didn't add faith into the mix.

In its simplest form, faith is taking God at His Word, and making it the final authority. Even when circumstances are contrary to the promise God has given, the individual who is operating in faith will continue trusting God's promise. Putting our trust in God's Word is very honoring to God because it is a declaration to Heaven that *God is good for His Word.*

It's not only saying He is trustworthy however, it's also a statement affirming He has the ability to bring about what He promised. This God who reveals Himself to us in the Word, who came in the flesh in His Son Jesus Christ, is not someone who gives empty promises - He has more than enough power to fulfil the promises He has given His children.

Summary

- When we're making the choice to believe the promises God makes in His Word regarding our situation, we're acting in faith.

- When we continue to stand on God's Word, trusting Him even when our circumstances are contrary to the promise, we're acting in faith.

- When we're faced with what may look like a 'giant' of financial debt, yet continue to believe God can help us, then we're walking by faith.

- When we believe God will help us clear our debt quicker than it would take 'naturally', then we're walking by faith.

"What is faith? It is the confident assurance that something we want is going to happen. It is the certainty that what we hope for is waiting for us, even though we cannot see it up ahead."

(Hebrews 11:1 (TLB)

Practical Exercise

It's important that a vision for financial freedom is based on God's promise, not wishful thinking or desire. Knowing what God has promised will birth the faith needed to see the vision fulfilled (Romans 10:17). Where in the Bible does God promise what you're believing for? You may need to use a concordance or the internet to find some verses. Write these verses out for yourself and refer back to them on a regular basis (even daily) – especially when things appear challenging. This way, you are watering the seed of faith that has been sown through the Word.

14

Praying Jesus' Way

Prayer is not about bringing a shopping list of needs to God. If my children only came to me when they needed something, I'd be disappointed. It would tell me they're only interested in what I can give them, not what I mean to them. God as a Father is no different, which is why prayer in its purest form is simply spending time with God in His presence. It's about enjoying God for who He is, and allowing Him to enjoy us. Every prayer time offers us the opportunity to praise God for who He is; thank Him for His faithfulness; as well as worship Him in spirit and truth[1].

There are advantages to following a routine during prayer times, but we need to guard against being prescriptive or dogmatic. We would soon find our circle of friends diminishing if every time we met with them, we had a rigid and inflexible 'conversation' that was one-sided. When we meet with God in prayer, we need to keep ourselves open to hearing His side of the conversation!

The most important thing about prayer is that there is a meeting of hearts - our heart with God's. Without a meeting of hearts, prayer becomes ritualistic, dull, and boring. It turns into a duty rather than a pleasure. When hearts come together however, the opposite happens. We come away refreshed and strengthened, having a new and clearer perspective of the day that's ahead of us. If we have a need, we can ask God to help us as part of the conversation we're having with Him. He already knows about it anyway[2], but still loves to hear us ask in the same way an earthly father wants to help his children when they ask.

Becoming debt-free is a need, so it's good to pray and ask God to help us get out of debt. When Jesus prayed, God heard all of His prayers[3], which means Jesus knew how to get results! He didn't keep the 'secret' of how to pray to Himself however, because at various times during His ministry He taught His followers some key things about prayer. If we can learn from the One who was so successful in prayer, and then *put into practice* what He's teaching us, the outcome will be that more of our prayers will be answered! The very reason Jesus taught on prayer was so that His followers would experience the same results He did. With that in mind, let's explore some of the things Jesus taught on how we should pray.

1. Ask!

There is a guarantee in Jesus' words when He tells us to ask. He says *"Ask, and it will be given to you; seek, and you will find; knock, and it will be opened to you. For everyone who asks receives, and he who seeks finds, and to him who knocks it will be opened"*[4]. There's no ambiguity in what Jesus teaches - He is clear that if we ask, we will get. I don't think I'm alone in saying that's not always our experience however. Sometimes we ask, but then don't see our prayers answered. Why is that?

The most important thing to remember when our prayers don't seem to get answered is that Jesus is still telling the truth, even though our *experience* may not line up with what He says. The trap we can fall into is allowing our experience to determine what we believe, rather than putting our trust in what Jesus says. What Jesus says is still true, even when our experience does not bear witness to it. That's because experiences can change, but the Word of God stands forever[5].

There are some things I've come to understand which have helped me make sense of why our prayers sometimes seem to go unanswered. One of these is that instead of asking from a position of confidence and faith, we'll ask God for things with a sense of unworthiness, thinking we don't deserve to have God answer our prayers. We think to ourselves *'I know how I've let God down and so why would He answer me?'*. One of the wonderful things about following Christ is that God answers prayer because He is gracious, not because we're good. If being deserving was one of the conditions for answered prayer, it would be a wage, not a gift from a loving Father. We would have *earned* our answer, whereas God wants to meet our needs out of His love, grace, and kindness towards us, not because we've earned it.

2. Seek the Intimacy of Relationship

Another common reason for not seeing answered prayer is that none of us truly know how good God is. Because of this, our expectations are lower than they should be when we're asking for something. Jesus had an intimate knowledge of what God was like as a Father[6], and it was out of His first-hand, *relational knowledge* that Jesus was able to approach God with such confidence and boldness. Jesus shared what He knew to be true with His followers, in order that they too could have the same confidence when they prayed.

Jesus taught how God is a perfect Father[7], far better than even the best earthly father anyone could have[8]. He also taught how God takes great delight in giving His children what He's promised[9]. This is a far cry from the image that God is somehow reluctant and unwilling to give us what we're asking for, and that we have to politely persuade Him to answer our prayer. This is a false image of God which Jesus dispels. It's because Jesus' relationship with God as a Father was so intimate that He was able to tell others the truth about what God is like. It's this personal knowledge of the Father that also gave Jesus the confidence to know His prayers would always be heard[10].

Jesus was teaching and demonstrating the goodness of God out of a place of *intimacy and relationship*, not out of a textbook. As we journey with God, if we spend time coming to know Him through prayer and reading the Bible, we'll come to experience what Jesus experienced - that God is loving, faithful, and extremely generous[11]. Knowing God for who He is will change us, as well as increase our faith and confidence for answered prayer. It is out of our *relationship* with Him that we'll come to know He is a caring Father. It's out of our *relationship* with Him that we'll come to trust His intentions towards us are always good. God the Father wants us to come to know Him for *ourselves*, not because someone else has told us[12]. This place of intimacy can only come through relationship, which means spending time with Him, not as a duty, but as an expression of our desire to know Him more deeply.

3. Receiving at the Point of Asking

One of the key principles Jesus taught His followers on prayer was how they need to receive what they've asked for at the point of asking, not when they see the request manifest in their lives. Jesus says "... *when you pray for something, believe that you have already received it. Then it will be yours*"[13]. Many people only believe they've had their prayers answered once they see it in the natural, whereas Jesus tells us to believe we've received the answer straight after we've asked for it. It doesn't require faith to believe God has answered our prayers once we see it manifest, because our senses (flesh) will bear witness to it. Believing God has answered our prayer *before* we see the answer however does require faith, because at that point we don't have any reason to believe, other than to trust that God is true to the promises He has given in His Word.

Again, the basis of being able to believe we've received what we've asked for, at the point of asking, comes from knowing the One we're praying to. Knowing God is faithful, trustworthy, and kind, brings a confidence that we've got what we've asked Him for. We won't need to wait for the answer before believing, because our heart will tell us He's heard our request[14]. *A personal heart-knowledge of God is the platform where faith and confidence can flourish.* Faith to see prayer answered is not the result of a formula, it is the unavoidable result of a relationship.

4. Avoid Empty Repetition

Jesus tells us not to *"recite the same prayer over and over as the heathen do, who think prayers are answered only by repeating them again and again. Remember, your Father knows exactly what you need even before you ask him"*[15].

Depending where our faith level is, we can find ourselves asking God for the same thing over and over again. God actually hears us the first time we ask[16], but because we don't have the confidence to believe He's heard us, we just keep on asking. Again, this points to how our faith to believe for the answer is based on seeing the request manifesting, rather than on what God has promised in His Word. We're leaning on our flesh, (our senses and natural understanding) in order to believe, rather than putting our faith and trust in God's faithfulness to deliver what He has promised.

If we take Jesus at His Word however, and trust that God has not only heard our prayer, but that the answer is also on its way[17], how we pray will change. The repetitiveness of asking for the same thing will be replaced by thankfulness, because we will have come to the place of knowing *in our hearts* that God has heard our prayers. It may be as we start off praying for someone or something in particular, we do find ourselves asking repeatedly, but once we come to the place of believing in our heart that God has heard us, we'll realize there's no need to keep asking. Knowing the answer is on its way will naturally lead us to begin thanking and praising God for His goodness, rather than continuing to ask.

In the parable of the widow and the unrighteous judge[18], Jesus taught how eager God is to answer prayer. Jesus didn't teach this parable to compare us to the widow, who had to constantly badger the one in authority so her request could be granted. Jesus' point in this parable was to reveal how God is *not like* the unrighteous judge, and so was encouraging the disciples to believe how God will answer prayer without delay, and without the need to be badgered[19]. It's a parable of *contrast* between God and the unrighteous judge, not a parable of *comparison* between us and the widow. In verse 8, Jesus brings clarity regarding why we can expect to have our prayers answered. It's when we approach the Righteous Judge *with faith*[20] - faith in what Jesus tells us about what God is like; faith in His goodness; as well as faith in God's faithfulness to deliver the promise He's given.

Summary

As we pray for God's help to get out of debt, we need to learn from Jesus regarding how to pray, and then trust that He knows what He's talking about. Jesus has a great track record in prayer and we would be foolish to ignore it. As we commit to seeking God's heart for ourselves, we will come to know *personally* that God is good, in exactly the way Jesus told us He is. It is a *personal knowledge* of God through relationship that brings us to the place of knowing for ourselves He is a loving and caring Father. This then gives us the confidence and faith to believe that when we ask, He hears us and will respond to the requests we've made.

The deeper we journey into God's heart, the less we seek things that gratify the flesh, because our heart wants to please Him and seek what He wants for our lives. Seeking a deeper relationship with God is what will save us from ourselves, because He places good desires on our hearts[21] - desires that cause us to prosper and flourish[22]. The joy of debt-freedom is one of the good desires God wants all of His children to experience, so let's continue to meet with God in prayer, and ask Him to lead us into it.

Prayer is a vital part of Christian life, whether we're in financial need or not. Take some time to consider the following questions, and be truthful with yourself regarding the answers.

1. Do you see prayer as a duty and an obligation, or as an opportunity to grow in your relationship with God as your Heavenly Father? Do you need to make changes in your prayer life that will help you seek God's *heart* as your priority, not His 'hand' (what He can give you)? What are those changes?

2. Do you trust what Jesus teaches about the nature and character of God as a Father? In what ways should that shape how you approach God to ask for His help?

3. Are you willing to ask God to help you trust His Word regarding what He's promised, rather than waiting to see the manifestation before you believe He's answered? If you are, then ask Him to help you with this.

15

We Bless God When We Tithe

Tithing is the act of giving the first ten percent of an income to God. Tithing is a fundamental part of God's financial system, not only is it the 'oil' that ensures God's church runs smoothly, tithing also sets in motion certain spiritual laws and principles that would otherwise remain dormant. As we look at the next few chapters and see what happens when a person tithes, we need to keep at the forefront of our minds that it's not necessarily the actual *giving* of the tithe that is the most important thing, but rather it is the *heart motivation* behind the tithe that is the crucial issue. Giving with a wrong attitude nullifies the blessing that is designed to follow the tithe, whereas the blessing is amplified when the tithe is given from a pure heart[1].

We *Worship* God as We Tithe

Tithing, the giving of the first ten percent, is an *act of worship* to God. By giving God the first, we're giving Him the best. Cain and Abel both brought an offering to God, yet only one was acceptable to Him[2]. We're told how *"After some time, Cain gathered some things he had grown. He brought them as an offering to the Lord,"* whereas Abel *"... also brought an offering. He brought the fattest parts of some animals from his flock. They were the first animals born to their mothers."*[3] Notice the difference - Cain brought his offering *'after some time'*, whereas Abel's offering

115

was *'the first animals born to their mothers'*. Cain had a look at what he had, then once he knew he had enough for himself, he gave out of what was left over. Abel on the other hand gave from the _first_ of every new-born, not knowing if, or how many more would be born. Abel's offering was an act of worship, from a heart that trusted and honored God as his Provider.

We *Honor* God as We Tithe

Tithing is an opportunity for us to *honor* God. Proverbs tells us *"Honor the Lord by giving him the first part of all your income, and he will fill your barns with wheat and barley and overflow your wine vats with the finest wines."*[4] When we honor someone, we're making the statement we hold them in high esteem, and have a great respect for them. We can honor God with our mouths, but then when we tithe the first of our income, it is the *practical* demonstration of what we're declaring with our words. Notice from these verses that there is a consequence to honoring God with our tithe - our needs are met in abundance. This happens as a natural consequence of honoring God first and foremost. It's something we cannot stop from happening because it is a spiritual law that God has hardwired into His financial system.

We *Bring Joy* to God as We Tithe

When we tithe, *it brings joy to God's heart* because it demonstrates we're trusting Him, not ourselves, as our Provider. Tithing is the opportunity to put the faith we're professing that God is our Provider into action. James tells us faith, without works, is dead[5]. When we're professing one thing, but then failing to demonstrate it through our actions, our faith becomes redundant. Tithing gives us the opportunity to bring our faith alive; it 'gives legs' to the faith we have so it can take us further along the road towards the financial destiny God has for us.

Our tithing blesses God's heart because it gives Him the opportunity to bless us in return. God takes great pleasure in seeing His children prosper, not only financially but in every area of life[6]. As we give Him our tithe, with it comes the demonstration that we trust Him. This is the green light He's waiting for to express His heart's desire to bless us. Tithing is not about God wanting our money, tithing is about God looking for the opportunity to bless us through our tithe!

Practical Exercise

If you are not already tithing your income to God, work out how much ten percent of your income would be, and make a note of it. Next to it, make a note of the ninety percent you would be left with if you made the decision to start tithing. Pray and ask God to give you a revelation about tithing in the light of these figures.

16

We Bless the Church When We Tithe

In the Old Testament, the worship and sacrificial system ordained by God through Moses was dependent on the tithing element of the system working properly. If the tithing element failed, the whole system would have collapsed.

The Levites were the tribe called by God to give their attention exclusively to making sure the worship system operated in the way God had commanded[1]. Unlike the other tribes, they were not given an inheritance of land following the conquest of Canaan, because God wanted their attention to be solely on ministering to Him[2]. By not giving them land, God was making sure the Levites wouldn't be distracted by having to work in the fields, or attend to any flocks as a means of providing for themselves and their families. The tithing system was God's way for providing for the Levites[3]. As the people brought their tithes and gave them to the Levites, it meant those who were ministering to God were being provided for. They were then free to give their undivided attention to the work they'd been called to. The Levites themselves were also required to tithe, so the tithing system was fair to everyone[4].

If the people had been disobedient to the command to bring the tithe, the Levites would have gone without. Their focus would then have needed to shift towards providing for themselves by other means. *The whole priestly system would have started to come apart at the seams if the people hadn't brought their tithes to the priests.* It is worth noting also that the tithes were not only there to provide for the Levites; what came in from the people's tithes was also meant to be used to help support widows, orphans, as well as the poor[5]. Through this Levitical system of tithing, God was giving a glimpse of how faithful He is to those who He calls to minister on His behalf; as well as the compassion He has towards those who are not able to provide for themselves.

The Shadow of Things to Come

The Tabernacle system in the wilderness, as well as the Temple system in Jerusalem were merely a 'shadow' of what was to come[6]. It was given as an earthly picture of what would be ushered in spiritually through Jesus Christ. Aaron, the high priest in the Tabernacle was a picture of the true High Priest to come - Jesus Christ[7]. We're also given another picture of Jesus as the High Priest in the account of Melchizedek, the king of Salem (Jerusalem)[8]. Abraham, or Abram as he was called at the time, brought a tenth of the spoils he had acquired when he rescued his nephew Lot, and gave his tithe to Melchizedek[9].

In the same way Abraham brought his tithe to the *'priest of God Most High'* (Melchizedek)[10]; we are now to bring our tithes to Jesus. Just like the Israelites brought their tithe to Aaron the high priest[11]; we are now to bring our tithes to our High Priest, Jesus. The way we do this is by bringing our tithe into God's 'storehouse' (the local church), so that there's 'food' in God's house[12]. As we bring our tithe, we are helping sustain those who like the Levites, are called by God to minister on His behalf[13]. The tithe is designed to support those who God calls out of secular employment, into His 'employment'. In the same way the tithe in the Levitical system was used to help support widows, orphans, and the poor, our tithe is also meant to be used for the same purpose today through the local church. The church has a responsibility to use part of the tithe to support compassion ministries that help the needy. Tithing is a blessing to God's church. It is a key part of God's system, ensuring those who have been called into full-time ministry are supported; helping meet the needs of the poor; as well as financing the propagation of the Good News of Jesus Christ. All these are important to God, and so as we bless the church with our tithes, we're also blessing Him.

Practical Exercise

You made a note earlier of how much your tithe would be. Take some time and ask God to show you the various ways this would make a difference to the local church you attend. Try to think about how it would be used if you decided to tithe - supporting staff, helping the poor, reaching out to people with the Gospel. Arrange to meet with someone who is in leadership in your church and ask them about how the tithes the people bring are used. Even if you are someone who is already tithing, it would be good for you to spend time understanding the huge difference your tithe makes to God's Kingdom.

17

We Bless Ourselves When We Tithe

We're blessing God's heart as we tithe; we bless the church as we tithe; but we're also blessing ourselves when we tithe! You may be thinking, *"How can ending up with less money be a blessing!"* Let me explain how giving the tithe blesses the individual.

The natural mind, which operates within the limits of reasoning and understanding, cannot comprehend how giving the first ten percent of our income is in any way a good thing[1]. It is no surprise therefore that the natural mind (the flesh) will try to persuade us not to[2]. God's financial system is not based on reasoning and understanding however, but is based on faith - faith in what God says. So, what does God say regarding the blessing that follows the person who tithes?

Tithing Leads to Increase

There is a *'cause and effect'* mechanism in God's financial system which can be seen throughout the Bible. In the Levitical system we looked at earlier, when the tithe was given to provide for the priests, the widow and orphan, as well as the poor, God promised He would bless the work of the hands of the one who was giving[3]. Everything the tither put their hand to would be blessed, which meant there was an increase over and above what they would have naturally been able to produce. As a result of this increase, more could be given to the priests; more was available to help the needy; and the remaining ninety percent for the individual was also greater. When we do things God's way, everybody benefits.

In the book of Proverbs, King Solomon wrote how the person who honors God with the *first* of their increase (the tithe), not only has plenty for themselves, but also an overflow to help others[4]. King Solomon also said *"Some people give freely and gain more; others refuse to give and end up with less"*[5]. The natural mind will reject this statement, simply because it cannot understand how giving away part of what we have will bring us more. Our part however is not to try to understand how it happens, but to receive *by faith* that it does, because it is what God has promised.

In sharing this wisdom, King Solomon knew what he was talking about. He was the richest, as well as the wisest earthly king Israel has ever known[6]. In writing these things, King Solomon was speaking out of what he knew to be true for himself, because it was his experience. It was God who revealed this wisdom to him[7], and by being obedient to the revelation he'd been given, he prospered in a greater way than has ever been seen since[8]. We would be foolish therefore to dismiss the wisdom of someone who has such a powerful testimony in the area of finances.

As we come towards the end of the Old Testament, the prophet Malachi also declares how a blessing follows the one who brings the tithe into God's 'storehouse'. He describes the blessing as God opening up the windows of heaven and pouring out a blessing of such magnitude that it cannot be contained[9].

Jesus Has Taken the Curse

In the verse previous to God promising to open up the windows of Heaven, we're told how withholding the tithe brings a curse, because it is robbing God of what is effectively His[10]. This begs the important question of whether the Christian who doesn't tithe is cursed or not? When a person chooses not to tithe, *God does not curse them.* That's because the *whole* of the curse has already been taken by Jesus Himself, on the Cross at Calvary. When a person's faith is in Jesus, the curse has no place in their lives, irrespective of their works[11]. However, the person who doesn't tithe is inadvertently making a statement that they don't trust God's system, and so by default are putting their faith in the only other system available to them - the world system. We saw earlier in the book how the world system is cursed, so effectively the person who doesn't tithe is choosing *for themselves* a system that is cursed. This is a far cry from thinking that God curses those who don't tithe, because He doesn't. God has left it to the individual to choose a financial system that is blessed, or one that is cursed[12].

Tithing Brings Spiritual Freedom

The greatest blessing tithing brings is not material, but *spiritual.* Making a commitment to tithe an income into God's storehouse takes faith, and with that faith comes spiritual freedom. The act of tithing releases the person from the spiritual bondage that money can bring, taking the individual into a place of spiritual freedom where they are trusting God as Provider, not their money. The anxiety or fear that may be felt initially when starting to tithe will eventually subside, because God's promise to faithfully provide will become an *experience*, not a theory. Somehow God makes the ninety percent that's left over after tithing, go further than the original hundred percent would have. This is a supernatural element of tithing that can only be experienced by those who tithe. Jill and I can personally testify to how true this is, as I'm sure countless others can also.

Tithing gives the individual the opportunity to demonstrate their love for God in a practical way[13]. It is a concrete way of demonstrating we are serious about making God's Kingdom and His righteousness first in our lives[14]. Our obedience is evidence of our love for God[15]. Unless we come to the place of trusting God as our Provider, we will never experience true freedom in the area of finances, no matter how much money we have. In fact, the more money we have, the more difficult it can become to hand things over to God and make Him our Provider.

This is partly what Jesus meant when He said it is more difficult for rich people to enter the Kingdom of God[16]. It is not that wealthy people are any less welcome; it's because riches can have a strong hold on people. The more money a person has, the more difficult it becomes to transfer their trust from something earthly and tangible, to Someone who is Spirit[17] - Someone who they can't see. No matter how much wealth an individual has, or how much of a hold the money has on them, there's still hope however. Jesus carries on by saying *"What is impossible for people is possible with God."[18]* If we desire to be set free from the hold money may have on us, no matter how strong that hold is, God can help us. All we need to do is ask, and He will give us His grace so that we can be set free[19]. Tithing is an opportunity for us to take a step towards financial spiritual freedom. If we take it, it will bring us closer to experiencing the fullness of the abundant life Jesus came to give us[20].

```
┌─────────────────────────────────┐
│        Practical Exercise        │
└─────────────────────────────────┘
```

In what ways would tithing your income benefit you as an individual? Ask God to show you the spiritual, as well as material benefits that would come to you personally as a result of tithing, and make a note of them below.

18

Tithing Reveals the Heart

Tithing is not as much a financial issue as it is a heart issue. Jesus says *"Wherever your treasure is, there the desires of your heart will also be"¹*. What we do with our money is governed by what is in our hearts. For example, if golf is our primary passion, then we will spend our time and money on things relating to golf - playing golf, watching golf, buying new golf clubs, golfing weekends etc. If our primary desire is to seek God and His Kingdom, then we'll naturally be generous towards the things of the Kingdom - both with our time and money. Where we direct our time and money is a reliable indicator of who (or what) has first place in our hearts. There is nothing wrong with enjoying golf or any other healthy pastime, but the Christian needs to be careful to make sure God's Kingdom and His righteousness has first place in their heart. In order to find, and then enjoy the abundant life Jesus came to give, God's Kingdom has to be our first priority².

It's possible to tithe for the wrong reasons. The trap of 'legalism' is real, where a person believes giving their tithe earns God's favor, and that God is pleased with them because they're tithing. This is what's known as a 'works' mentality, where the individual thinks it is their effort that makes them right with God. Tithing with a works mentality nullifies the grace of God, and even though it will materially benefit the church, we ourselves will miss out on the blessing the tithe is designed to bring. This is because the person is depending on their own works, rather than faith in Christ as their source of righteousness[3]. Another wrong motive for tithing is fear - the fear of coming under God's judgement for not tithing. Hopefully what was shared in the previous chapter regarding how God does not curse nor condemn the individual who doesn't tithe will allay any fears that may have arisen.

Tithe with a Smile

What then is the correct attitude towards tithing? Imagine someone standing in front of you with the biggest smile you've ever seen. That's what our hearts should look like when we're giving to God. The apostle Paul tells us *"You must each decide in your heart how much to give. And don't give reluctantly or in response to pressure. "For God loves a person who gives <u>cheerfully.</u>""[4]* The Greek word for 'cheerfully' is *'hilarōs'*[5], which is where the English word *hilarious* is derived from. Paul tells us we're not to give reluctantly, nor are we to give if we feel pressured in some way, but rather to give *cheerfully*. God is blessed by the heart that is *pleased* to give, irrespective of how much the actual tithe is[6]. The person who gives with a smile on their hearts *wants* to give; they *enjoy* giving; and are *pleased* to give. The blessing that follows the tithe comes to the individual who gives with the right heart attitude - the one who gives cheerfully.

A voluntary, cheerful approach has always been what God is looking for from His people. When the Tabernacle was being built during the Israelites' time in the wilderness, God instructed Moses to *"tell the Israelites to bring me gifts. You will accept gifts for me from everyone <u>who is willing</u> to give"*[7]. There was no compulsion to give, but there was an opportunity for those who wanted to honor God, to do so through their giving.

Today in the church there is no compulsion to give, but for those who want to honor God so that the work of His Kingdom can be extended, one of the opportunities presented to them is through giving the tithe cheerfully.

The Grace of God Enables Tithing

Tithing in the Old Testament was a lawful requirement - the people were *commanded* to tithe in line with the Law given through Moses[8]. The Christian is no longer under the Law, but under grace[9]. Grace however doesn't *take away* the responsibility to tithe, in fact, grace does the complete opposite. God's grace *enables* the individual who desires to walk righteously with God to tithe cheerfully. Grace is given to us as a gift by God because of our faith in Christ[10], it is the 'supernatural fuel' that enables the individual to do the things God has called them to do, which includes tithing[11].

Under the Old Covenant (the Law), the people were *commanded* not to murder, *commanded* not to steal, *commanded* not to commit adultery. Being under God's grace doesn't suddenly take away the Christian's responsibility not to murder, not to steal, nor to commit adultery. Neither does grace take away the responsibility to tithe! The wonderful thing about grace is that it circumcises the heart of the believer, taking away the old nature that was inclined to murder, steal, and commit adultery[12]. But grace doesn't stop there, because once the old nature is dealt with, grace then carries on its work and gives the individual a *new* heart. This new spiritual heart desires to be obedient to God's way of doing things and is enabled to do so, because God has written His *'law of love'* on it[13].

The Christian who is truly born-again no longer has to be *commanded* not to murder, because as a result of grace they have been given a heart that is now able to pray, as well as show mercy towards their enemies[14]. The born-again Christian no longer has to be *commanded* not to steal, because the new heart they have been given wants to give to others, not take from them. This is true even when they've been treated badly by others[15]. It is the same with tithing. The born-again Christian no longer has to be *commanded* to tithe, because the radical change that has taken place in their heart as a result of God's grace, means they're now free to cheerfully and willingly honor God with their finances. Christ calls on His followers to go *beyond*, or *higher* than the Old Testament Law[16]. Grace is the gift of God that enables the Christian to be obedient to that call.

The Unbelieving or Reluctant Spouse

What if an individual desires to tithe, but their spouse is not in agreement? Even when both are Christians, one spouse may want to tithe while the other resists. Or it could be a Christian is married to an unbelieving spouse. Either way, how should they proceed if one spouse is not in agreement with tithing?

Unity in marriage is a priority for God, and so a Christian who wants to tithe, but has a spouse who is in opposition, should not go ahead regardless. There are a number of approaches that can be considered when it is only one spouse who wants to tithe.

The priority in such situations is to come to a place of agreement, which usually involves compromise on both sides, similar to any other area of financial expenditure that married couples have to agree on. It may be that agreement can be reached on making a regular and fixed contribution to support the activities of the church. Another possibility is that if the married couple each have their own personal allowance apportioned every month, then the spouse who wants to tithe can do so out of their own allowance. Even when the one who wants to tithe is the main breadwinner, it should not be done without the consent and agreement of both parties.

Because tithing is primarily a heart issue, *the heart desire to tithe* is the most important thing to God, not the mechanics of it. Even though there may be reasons to compromise for the sake of unity in marriage, if the desire to tithe is present, God sees their heart[17]. When an individual finds themselves in a situation where it's not easy to tithe because of the constraints of marriage, they should also seek the counsel of their Pastor who is ideally placed to understand their particular situation.

Don't Delay

Early on in my Christian walk, in trying to encourage a friend who was hesitant about tithing, I suggested he start with a smaller percentage and work his way up to the full ten percent. I was completely wrong to suggest this as a solution, and thankfully I was corrected almost immediately by a more mature believer. The tithe is ten percent, anything less in not a tithe, even if it is nine-point nine percent. Tithing is an act of faith, and if we start 'tithing' at a lower level where it seems affordable, it doesn't require faith and so becomes a 'works'. It is faith that pleases God, and it is faith that brings the blessing that follows tithing[18].

Waiting until we think we can afford to tithe is a missed opportunity, because we're unlikely to start tithing at all if we do this[19]. Tithing needs to start even when we don't know how things will 'add up' for us, because it's a statement of how we are trusting God and His financial system, not what we see on paper. If God is speaking into our heart about tithing, and we sense a desire to start, God will lead us to the 'when and how' if we're prepared to ask Him for direction. Because tithing is ultimately a heart issue, if we're willing to open our heart to God and invite Him to change us, that in itself is a huge step towards the financial, and spiritual freedom we're seeking. God is not after our money, He is after our heart. As we give Him the *whole* of our heart, which includes what we do with our money, we will walk into the complete freedom He longs for us to enjoy.

Practical Exercise

Is there anything holding you back from tithing? Ask God to reveal any areas of insecurity, doubt, or fear you may have, and ask Him to set you free from them. If you are still not at the place where you feel you can tithe, talk to someone in leadership at your church and ask them to pray with you about the situation. Don't push the issue of tithing to one side by ignoring or forgetting about it. It is such an integral part of God's financial system that it demands a response if we're going to walk into the fullness of what God has in store for us.

19

Going Beyond the Tithe

Christians are called to be generous over and above the tithe[1]. Some see this as a joy and a privilege, others see it as a burden. Once again, it all depends on the condition of the heart. Christian giving is not designed to be burdensome, because Jesus promises the 'yoke' He places on His followers is easy, and the responsibilities He gives them are light[2]. Therefore, if we find it difficult to give, we need to pause and take stock. We need to ask God *"Why is helping others out of my finances causing me anxiety, and not bringing me the joy You promised?"*. We need to be honest with God and ask Him to search our hearts[3], revealing what is hindering us from experiencing the blessing that giving is meant to bring[4].

Every Christian should be generous; it is simply a reflection of their heavenly Father[5]. Some Christians are also given the *spiritual gift* of giving, where they are led by the Holy Spirit to first of all recognize a specific need, and then to meet that need out of the resources they have[6]. There are still others who have a *ministry* of giving. The main focus of their calling is to generate financial resources, and then distribute them according to God's leading[7]. These 'Kingdom Distributors' help support people, projects, and events financially, so that the work of the Kingdom of God can move forward[8].

Sowing and Reaping

God has put in place a *natural,* as well as a *spiritual* law that whatever a man sows, he will also reap[9]. We see this law working in the natural realm when a farmer sows seed for a crop, ending up with a harvest that is a lot more than the seed sown. This law of sowing and reaping also operates in the *spiritual* realm, because Jesus said when we 'sow' judgement on others (as an example), the harvest of judgement that comes back to us is far greater[10]. Reaping what we sow is a *law* - both in the natural as well as the spiritual realm, which means it is *unchangeable*. Being ignorant of it, or choosing not to believe there is such a law in operation does not make us exempt. The law of gravity works exactly the same for the person who is aware of it, as it does for the person who doesn't know about it. We know that because stepping off a tall building brings the same result for both. Similarly, the law of sowing and reaping is in operation whether we know about it or not.

Learning From the Farmer

Farmers understand the various principles needed to bring a good harvest from the seed they sow. By looking at what a farmer does in the *natural* realm, it's possible to glean some understanding about how sowing and reaping works in the *spiritual* realm. Appreciating the principles involved equips us to make good choices, because we'll be aware how important it is to sow good things, so that we reap good things (love, kindness, and joy are examples). The law of sowing and reaping is already in place, it is fixed and unchangeable[11]. Our responsibility is to make sure we understand how it works, and then *work with it* for our own good, as well as for the good of others.

Seed Needs to be Sown

The first and most obvious thing a farmer knows to do is *sow the seed*. No farmer will leave their seed in a bag in the barn and then expect a harvest! *They know they have to sow their seed in order to produce a harvest,* and if they haven't sown seed for any reason, no amount of hoping and wishing will bring them one. It is the same when it comes to God's financial system, the Christian cannot expect to reap a harvest if they haven't sown seed by being generous towards others. Keeping all our money in a bank or building society, thereby ignoring the needs of others will not produce a harvest[12].

Look for Good Ground

The second important principle a farmer looks at is *where* they sow their seed. They won't just sow seed anywhere, because they know the harvest is directly related to the quality of the soil. Poor soil cannot produce the harvest that good soil can, so making sure they sow into good soil is critical. This is also true for the Christian who is giving money. Because there are so many different ministries, charities, and individuals someone can give to, it's important to prayerfully ask God where He wants them to direct their money so that their seed lands on good ground. It is in good soil that seed produces thirty, sixty, and a hundredfold return[13].

A Balanced Approach

The farmer also knows that the harvest they produce will be proportionate to the *amount* of seed they sow. If they only sow a handful of seed in the corner of a field, they know not to expect a bumper crop that fills the whole field! Similarly, if they sow sufficient seed to cover the whole field, they will rightly expect a greater harvest. It is no different for the Christian who is following God's principles of sowing and reaping. In the context of writing to the church about money, the apostle Paul says *"The one who plants only a little will gather only a little. And the one who plants a lot will gather a lot"*.[14]

We need to make sure we get this into perspective however. In teaching about giving to others, Paul also adds *"I don't mean that others should have relief while you have hardship. Rather, it's a matter of striking a balance."*[15] We are to give out of what we have, not out of what we don't have[16]. Our heart may want to give more than we're able to, which in itself is good, but we need to mix our giving with wisdom and faith. The wisdom is recognizing God is not asking us to give to the point we're neglecting the other responsibilities we have[17]. The faith part is to believe that, because our heart is in the right place, God will eventually get more to us so that the desire of our heart to give more can be fulfilled[18].

Avoid Wrong Motives

Understanding the principle of how sowing money brings in a harvest has unfortunately led some to give for the wrong reasons, because they fall into the trap of thinking it's a 'formula'. When someone gives money with the primary intention of gaining more money for themselves, it is clear the attitude of the heart is wrong. When this happens, they are being driven by their selfish nature, wanting to fulfil the desires of what their flesh wants. In doing this, the individual will receive a harvest, but not necessarily the one they're hoping for.

By sowing selfishness, they will unwittingly reap selfishness. They will then become increasingly frustrated when they don't see the financial harvest they expected, and may well move on to some other 'money-making' endeavor because that's where the treasure of their hearts is[19].

For the person whose heart is set on the Kingdom of God as a first priority[20], giving money ('sowing') will cause God to move on their behalf and bring in a harvest greater than the seed they sowed. God knows He can trust them with the resources He is blessing them with. Here again, we see how the attitude of the heart is the critical element God is looking for[21]. Allowing God to change our hearts so that our motives are pure and reflect His heart's desire, is what will bring us a harvest following our sowing. When this happens, the same heart attitude will then want to give more of what they've received towards helping others, thus sowing more seed for a future harvest. Sowing and reaping soon becomes a lifestyle, where the individual truly experiences Jesus' promise that it is more blessed to give than to receive[22].

A Farmer Knows What to Expect

At Creation, God made sure all the trees and plants would produce seed, in order for them to naturally reproduce. There was no need for Him to re-visit creation because He'd 'programmed' new growth to come through the seeds that would be produced. The seeds from every plant or tree *"would produce the kind of plants and fruit they came from"*[23]. It is obvious that the seed from a plant or tree will only generate the same kind of tree or plant it comes from. An acorn will only grow into an oak tree, similarly apple seeds will only grow into apple trees, and so on. This is why farmers can plan their harvest. Depending on the crop they want, they sow the seed accordingly. Once they've sown the seed for a crop of wheat, they're not then anxiously waiting to see if carrots come up!

The farmer knows they're guaranteed that having sown wheat, it is wheat they will get.

Even though this is an obvious principle when it comes to sowing and reaping, many people ignore it and continue to 'sow' negative things in their lives, yet resent the harvest they get in return. When an individual displays anger towards other people for example, the harvest they will reap is other people being angry with them. Similarly, when someone is unfaithful, they will find other people being unfaithful to them, constantly letting them down. Jesus makes this point very clearly in His teaching[24], as does the apostle Paul when he says *"Don't be fooled. You can't outsmart God. A man gathers a crop from what he plants"*[25]. We cannot *change* the laws of sowing and reaping that God has instituted, either in the natural or spiritual realm. The best and wisest thing to do therefore is to first of all *understand* this law, and then to *work with it* so we are able to control the harvest that comes back to us.

God has created the law of sowing and reaping so that man can benefit from it[26]. It is therefore essential we co-operate with this law in a way that brings the blessings God has planned for us to have. We need to avoid reaping the negative consequences that come as a result of ignorance or unbelief. Because *"whatever a man sows, this he will also reap"*[27], in the context of this book dealing with finances, it means giving money will bring in a harvest of money. When we appreciate money can be a seed, and that God has arranged things so that every seed reproduces after its own kind[28], it is not unreasonable to expect a harvest when we give money to help others, *provided the motivation of the heart is right.*

Is there a danger of simply 'hoping and wishing' God will help us to get out of debt, without actually engaging *practically* with His financial system? Even if you're only able to give a little to start with, ask God to show you who you can help with the seed you have in your hand. Then take the step of giving it, so that you begin to engage practically with God's law of *whatever a man sows, that he will also reap.*

20

Growing a Harvest

No farmer will sow seed one day, and then go out the next day expecting a harvest. They know there is a season for sowing, and then after a period of time, a season for harvesting what has grown. That's because the seed needs to first of all germinate; then produce the first blade; and then grow to reach full maturity. Only then can it be harvested[1]. There are certain things a farmer can do to *help* the growing process, but one thing they can't do is by-pass the various stages of development needed to bring a harvest.

It is the same when a Christian gives money in faith, out of a good heart. They sow the 'seed', but it then takes time for the seed to germinate and grow, so that it brings a harvest. During the time between sowing and seeing the harvest, there is a need to be patient, which involves perseverance, especially when it looks like there is nothing happening on the surface! The apostle Paul tells us not to grow weary as we wait for the harvest, but to continue to do what is right as we wait[2]. Like the farmer, we shouldn't be worrying about what's happening to the seed we've planted, but continue to believe it's growing even when we can't see any evidence on the surface[3]. How a plant grows to something hundreds of times bigger than the seed it came from is a mystery, yet it happens. How the seed of money grows into something much bigger than what was sown is also a mystery, but that is how God has created the law of sowing and reaping in His financial system.

Allowing The Seed to Die

When a seed is sown into the ground, it first of all needs to die before it can produce a harvest[4]. Similarly, when we sow money into a church, a ministry, or to an individual, we need to let it 'die' so it can produce a harvest. From the moment we give money as a gift, we need to recognize it ceases to be our money because it has become someone else's possession. It is wrong to use a 'gift' as leverage in an attempt to influence or coerce the recipient to act in our favor. It's okay to explain we're giving towards a particular project or need, but trying to influence through giving a gift is called bribery! In giving money as a gift, it's as we let go of it that it dies, so that it then is able to bring a harvest.

Don't Eat All Your Seed!

During the pre-industrial days of farming when seed couldn't be bought, farmers would keep some seed back from what they harvested, knowing they would need it for the following year. Eating all their seed by making bread, or using it for food would mean they would have no seed left to sow. No seed to sow would have meant no crop to harvest. No crop to harvest would mean the farmer and their family would be looking at an empty field, which would have been disastrous.

The same principle applies to money. We need to be careful not to spend everything we receive on ourselves, because we'll end up with no seed to sow for the next harvest. We're meant to enjoy spending income on ourselves, but we're also given enough by God as seed to sow for a future harvest. This is how the apostle Paul explains it, referring to the 'bread' as what we keep and use for ourselves: *"God is the one who gives seed to plant and bread to eat. He will give you enough to give away and will make it become more and more. Of the good things you do he will give you a big harvest"*[5]. We're meant to enjoy what God generously gives us, but we're also called to be wise and not to use all of it on ourselves, but rather to put some aside as seed so we can sow for our next harvest.

Keeping the Harvest 'Disease Free'

If a crop is going to produce its maximum yield for harvesting, it needs to be disease-free. Leaf blotch, fruit flies, and other plant infections have the potential to drastically reduce or even decimate a crop. Similarly, there are certain things that can reduce the harvest that follows sowing money, so we'll take a few moments to consider what some of these are.

Pride

If an individual gives money with a prideful heart, it will kill the crop. The symptoms of a prideful heart are wanting others to either see, or to know about their giving. They will boast, sometimes subtly, about who they're helping, and how much they're giving.

Jesus warned against a prideful attitude when giving to others, saying our giving needs to be 'in secret'[6]. In Jesus' time, the Pharisees made a public display of their giving, wanting everybody to see so they could appear 'holy', looking for the respect of the people. Jesus explained the reward that comes from this prideful, public giving is limited to the acknowledgement and praise of the people only. That is the extent of their reward, because God is not able to bless the giving of an individual who is motivated by pride.

The Christian needs to adopt a low profile when they give, to the extent that Jesus compares it to the left hand not knowing what the right hand is doing[7]. It is this kind of giving that gets God's attention[8]. Those who take this humble approach will not only be rewarded financially, but are promised God's help when they need it[9]. They're also promised that God will teach them His way of doing things[10]; and that they'll freely receive His grace[11], wisdom[12], and honour[13]. Humility is a big deal in God's Kingdom, and so there is a need for it to be reflected in our giving. We need to strive to be free from all pride, otherwise it will negate the fruitfulness of what God wants us to receive. This fruitfulness is not just material, but also spiritual, because humility opens the door to the joy and excitement that giving is meant to bring.

Injustice

The prophet Micah is someone else we can learn from with regard to making sure our harvest remains disease-free. Micah tells us what God expects from His people - *"You must act with justice. You must love to show mercy. And you must be humble as you live in the sight of your God"*[14]. A few verses later Micah tells us what happens if we don't follow God's advice; *"You will plant your seeds, but you will not gather food. You will try to squeeze oil from your olives, but you will not get any oil. You will crush your grapes, but you will not get enough juice to have wine to drink"*[15].

Being unjust towards others; failing to be merciful to those around us; and a failure to walk humbly with God (i.e. living pridefully) will all destroy any harvest we're hoping to reap.

Impatience

Another 'disease' that can affect our harvest is *impatience*. We touched on this earlier in the chapter, but it is worth highlighting again that every seed needs time to germinate, to grow, and then to mature before it is able to bring a harvest. It's impossible for us to make the seed grow, so we have to leave it to God. Our part is to trust God will do what He promised (which is supernatural), and as we wait, to be patient and continue to persevere no matter how trying our circumstances may appear[16]. Seeing financial increase from sowing money as seed is a matter of faith, not what can be seen in the natural[17]. The frustration that comes from being impatient can easily lead to speaking negatively about our situation, which can adversely affect the harvest because our words carry power. This is what we will move on to look at in the next chapter.

Carry out a *'spiritual heart check'* with regard to your giving by checking the following areas:

- Do you allow your seed to 'die' when you give to someone, or do you have a tendency to hold on to it by trying to influence the recipient in some way?

- Is there any evidence of pride in your giving? Do you like people to know you are a giver? If so why, and what can you do to change? (James 4:6; 1 Peter 5:5).

- Ask God to show you any attitudes of heart that may be affecting your harvest. This is not so you can feel condemned, but so that you can deal with them and see an increased harvest.

21

Watering the Seed

Everyone knows how seed needs to be watered before it can start to germinate. As the plant grows, it continues to need water if it's going to develop into a healthy, mature plant which produces lots of fruit. A lack of water will hold a crop back and even lead to a complete failure. It's clear therefore that water is an essential requirement for a fruitful harvest.

It is no different when it comes to sowing the 'seed' of money. Once sown, it needs to be constantly watered, otherwise the anticipated harvest will be disappointing. But how do we water the 'seed' of money? Very simply - with our words.

God tells us: *"Rain and snow fall from the sky and don't return until they have watered the ground. Then the ground causes the plants to sprout and grow, and they produce seeds for the farmer and food for people to eat. In the same way, my words leave my mouth, and they don't come back without results. My words make the things happen that I want to happen. They succeed in doing what I send them to do"*[1].

In these verses from Isaiah, God first of all draws our attention to something we understand in the *physical realm*. We're reminded how the rain and snow are sent to water the ground, producing seed for the farmer to grow plants to eat. God then tells us that *exactly* the same thing happens spiritually with the words that come out of His mouth (referring to His Word, the

Bible). If we look closely, God is saying in these verses that His words bring a harvest which never fails. If we are willing to give voice to God's Word *by speaking it out of our mouths*, it will have the same effect as rain has on natural plants - it will cause His promises to come about and we will reap the harvest of what God has said. This is not a mechanical exercise however, because it is essential to mix our confession of God's Word with faith[2] - faith in God's faithfulness, as well as faith in God's ability to bring about what He has promised.

My prayer is that for those who don't already understand the important role words play in determining a person's future, that God will bring His revelation to that person. Unfortunately, the great majority of people do not understand how powerful their words are in shaping their destiny. That's because this is a *spiritual* principle, which means it's outside what the natural mind can grasp or understand[3]. When an individual either ignores or resists the spiritual truth of how powerful words are, they are in danger of shaping their future with negative, destructive words; words that are outside the will of God for their lives[4].

Biblical Evidence that Words Carry Power

This chapter is not meant to be an exhaustive study on the effect our words have on shaping our lives. But there is a need to highlight some Biblical examples that clearly demonstrate this spiritual truth. We need to understand how the words we speak affect the harvest we receive from the seed we sow. It's essential for us to know this spiritual law exists, and then to make any necessary adjustments so that we're making sure the law is working in our favor, not to our detriment.

Joshua

God appointed Joshua to lead His people into the Promised Land[5]. The Israelites were about to face some fierce battles, so the Lord instructed Joshua on the way forward. He told Joshua: *"This Book of the Law shall not depart from your mouth, but you shall meditate on it day and night, so that you may be careful to do according to all that is written in it; for then you will make your way prosperous, and then you will achieve success"*[6]. Joshua was instructed to meditate on God's Word, to be obedient to it, and then *to speak it out his mouth*! If he would do that, God promised He would give the Israelites success and prosper them. Joshua took God's instruction literally, because later in the battle to take Canaan we read how Joshua's *words* caused the sun and moon to stop their natural pattern for a day[7]. Influencing natural events with words spoken in faith is also seen in the New Testament. Jesus did the same thing with a storm, using His *words* to bring calm[8].

King Solomon

We've acknowledged King Solomon's wisdom earlier in the book, so it's worth listening to what he has to say about the effect our words can have. There are a number of verses in Proverbs that talk about the 'tongue' (referring to the words we speak), but I'm limiting it here to just one of the things Solomon says. *"Death and life are in the power of the tongue, and they who indulge in it shall eat the fruit of it [for death or life]"*[9].

The wisest earthly king of Israel tells us how the tongue, (the words we speak), carries life, or death. We know from personal experience how negative words can affect us. Even words from our childhood can still have an effect on us as adults if we allow them to. Conversely, affirming and positive words have the opposite effect - they build us up. This is how powerful words are, and King Solomon tells us that we will 'eat' the consequences of the words we speak.

When we speak negative words about ourselves or our situation, we're inviting that to become our future[10]. When we speak affirming and positive words however, that then becomes our future. The important thing to remember is that God is not asking us to simply make up our own words to speak over ourselves - but to speak what He has already spoken over us, which is now ours because of our faith in Christ. It's the future God has planned for us we need to be pursuing with our words, which is why we need to first of all meditate on what God says in His Word. We are then able to come into agreement with it in our hearts, finally speaking it out of our mouths. As we do this, we're giving God's Word a voice to influence our personal situation[11].

Jesus

There are many more examples in the Old Testament which demonstrate the spiritual law that words carry power, but we need to move on to look at the One who demonstrated the power of words to the uttermost - Jesus during His earthly ministry. With His _words_, Jesus healed sick bodies[12]. With His _words_, Jesus delivered the demon-possessed[13]. With His _words_, Jesus raised the dead[14]. With His _words_, Jesus changed the course of nature just as Joshua did[15]. Jesus calls us as His followers to use our words in the same way[16], teaching us that by using something spiritual, we can influence the material, physical realm.

Even if we can't see ourselves at the moment speaking to a mountain and casting it into the sea as Jesus teaches us to, we need to know with absolute certainty that our words carry the power of death and life. The minimum we need to do therefore is to make sure we control what comes out of our mouths, tailoring our words so that we're bringing them in line with what God has declared over us in His Word. Like King David, who understood this law very well, we need to ask God *"Lord, help me control what I say. Don't let me say anything bad"*[17].

Watering Our Seed with God's Word

Hopefully the examples we've just looked at will help us understand how from a Biblical perspective, the words we speak carry the power of 'life and death'. What we choose to speak - whether life or death - will be what we experience in life[18]. Once we know this truth, how do we then apply it so that our words take us towards the good future God has promised for us?[19] The answer is very simple - it is by *confessing*, or *speaking out what God has already spoken over us.*

God has got every base covered with regard to the needs we have in life. If the need is for healing, for freedom, for peace, or for restoration (as examples), there is a promise for it somewhere in the Bible. There is a condition however to having our needs met by God, which is we need to be "in Christ". It is as a person surrenders their heart and life to Christ that God places them 'in Christ'. Once in Christ, God can then meet every need of the individual, because all of what God has promised in His Word is ours because of what Christ has done[20].

With regard to the financial needs we have, it's important to locate the promises God has made regarding financial provision, then to start confessing them, or speaking them out over ourselves. That's when we're watering the ground of our hearts so that the Seed of the Word of God can grow[21], as well as watering any material seed we have sown financially. Confessing God's Word is not an attempt to persuade God to do something on our behalf, because He already has....in Christ. Confessing God's promises over our lives is simply *coming into agreement* with what God has already promised us. God doesn't need persuading, because His mind is already made up, which is why He spoke the promises in the first instance!

Once we have taken the step of sowing our money as seed, we then need to make sure we water it by speaking the promises of God over it. That's when it will start to produce what God wants it to produce. God has promised that the words that come out of His mouth *"...will not return to me without producing results. They will accomplish what I want them to. They will do exactly what I sent them to do"*[22]. God is on our side. Let's take Him at His Word by speaking and declaring what He has promised over our lives. As we do that, the law of sowing and reaping will be working in our favor, bringing us the crop we're looking for when harvest time arrives![23]

Practical Exercise

Ask God to show you whether you're speaking negative words over yourself or your family, words that are not in line with what He has promised you in His Word. Take time to listen to Him, then ask for His help by praying verse 3 in Psalm 141. Then look for Scripture verses that declare His will for you regarding finances, and start speaking those over your life on a regular basis so that you are moving into the future God has planned for you in Christ.

22

The Simplicity of God's Financial System

Before we move on to the final part of the book which deals with the *practical aspects* of stewardship, I believe it would be good to briefly highlight how simple God's financial system really is. The best way to do this is to look at some verses from the apostle Paul's second letter to the church at Corinth, which condenses the essence of God's system into a few verses.

Paul deals with issues relating to money over two chapters, (2 Corinthians chapters 8 & 9), but I believe the particular verses highlighted provide a fitting summary of how God's system works. The verses below are taken from the Worldwide English (New Testament) (WE) version, and are followed by what I believe Paul is trying to communicate in these verses. If you wish, you can take time over the next few days or weeks to meditate on a verse each day so that the truth of God's Word regarding finances is given the opportunity to root, and then to grow in your heart[1].

2 Corinthians 9:7-11 (WE)

"7 Everyone should give what he wants in his heart to give. He should be glad to give it, and should not give it because he was forced to give. `God loves a person who gives gladly.' 8 God is able to give you even more blessings than you need. In all things you will always have all you need for yourselves, and you will have enough to help all others. 9 The holy writings say, `A good man gives away many things. He

gives to the poor people. He will always be a good man in the sight of God.' ¹⁰ God is the one who gives seed to plant and bread to eat. He will give you enough to give away and will make it become more and more. Of the good things you do he will give you a big harvest. ¹¹ You will become rich in every way. And then you will have enough to give plenty to all people. And many people will thank God for your gifts which we will bring them".

1. The attitude of the heart is the most important aspect of giving as far as God is concerned. We need to ask God to replace *'the heart that wants to get'*; with *'a heart that wants to give'*. (Verse 7)

2. God's promise is that when we work with Him, He has the power to make sure we are provided for, as well as having an excess to help others. (Verse 8)

3. The righteousness we're given as a gift through faith in Christ will shine through us and will be evidenced as we give to the poor. (Verse 9)

4. Ultimately, everything we have comes from God. He gives us what we need to live on ('bread'); as well as 'seed' so we can give to others. Provided we use our seed in the way He has prescribed, we'll always get a harvest back on it. (Verse 10)

5. As we give out of the excess God gives us, we prosper in every area of life. The kindness we show to people, our generosity, as well as the joy we have in helping others will all increase, together with our finances. People will thank God for us. (Verse 11)

Moving Forward with God

When a Christian gives *with a right heart attitude,* God promises to supply all their needs, as well as providing an overflow so they can help others. This is what Scripture teaches[2]. Our personal views on money, a lack of Biblical understanding where finances are concerned, or even possibly wrong teaching in the past can all be stumbling blocks to the truths God shares in His Word about money. I would therefore encourage every individual to humble themselves before God, and ask Him whether there are any wrong attitudes which may be hindering them from receiving the revelation of truth regarding Biblical finances. Truth stands on its own - it doesn't need anyone's approval or agreement for it to be truth. *This means God will not change His truths to accommodate an individual's wrong perceptions.* It's imperative for us to press into the truth of what God has already said, and ask Him with humility and faith for the revelation of truth He has promised to give[3]. Let's not miss the blessings He has prepared for us to enjoy because of ignorance[4], pride[5], or lack of understanding[6]. Let's not allow any preconceptions or strongholds that may have developed over the years to become a barrier to His goodness and grace. We cannot afford to miss the truth of what God wants us to know about finances - either for our own sake, or the sake of others who God wants to bless through us[7].

God's Financial Cycle

Receive what God gives with a grateful heart, because He is kind & generous.

Give tithes and offerings (gifts) from a cheerful, thankful heart.

Believe God's promise for a return so that the cycle can start all over again.

Take time to look at the verses shared in this chapter from 2 Corinthians 9:7-11. Ask God to show you if there are any areas of ignorance, misconception, or unbelief that are preventing you from entering into the fulness of what He has for you, and then deal with them. Ask Him to reveal to you the *simplicity* of His financial system, as well as give you the grace (the ability) to operate within it.

(This is the last 'Practical Exercise' that appears at the end of each chapter. Because the final part of the book deals with the practical aspects of stewardship, the practical exercises are effectively contained within the chapters themselves).

'All that you do must be done in love'.

1 Corinthians 16:14

Part 4

Practical Stewardship

23

Growing as Stewards

The primary emphasis of the book so far has been on the *spiritual* aspect of becoming debt-free. In this final part of the book, the focus shifts to the *practical* aspects of how to deal with finances. The starting point is to understand the Biblical principle of what it means to be a steward.

What is Stewardship?

In its simplest form, stewardship can be regarded as taking responsibility for, and then managing someone else's property. Stewardship is a relationship between two parties. On the one hand the *owner* is willing to trust the one they're asking to look after and manage their affairs for them. Then on the other side of the relationship, the one who is called to be a *steward* demonstrates they are faithful with what they have been given. How a steward deals with what they've been given is key to the relationship, because if they can't show themselves to be trustworthy, the owner will obviously look for someone else to manage their affairs.

These principles are the foundation of Biblical stewardship - whether it relates to finances, or any other gift or talent God gives a person. Everything that is good in our lives is a gift from God[1], and even though God will not take back His gifts[2], He does expect us to be good stewards of what we're given. As we demonstrate our faithfulness, a number of things happen.

First of all, the Kingdom of God is expanded. This is because the proper use of our gifts and talents enables more and more people to encounter the love of Jesus Christ[3]. Secondly, the church is built up and made stronger[4]. Thirdly, the fruit which comes from using our gifts brings glory to God[5]. Lastly, demonstrating we're able to produce fruit with what we've been given allows God to give us more responsibility[6]. What all this means is that stewardship is a serious matter, because if we fail to use either our spiritual or material gifts correctly, each and every one of those areas will suffer.

A Steward is Free from an 'Ownership Mentality'

The biggest challenge to a healthy attitude towards stewardship is having an 'ownership' mentality. Many Christians struggle with the concept that everything they have, including their finances, is God's. This is because they feel *they* are the ones who have gone out to work and earned it. We need to remember however that *every* good gift comes from God[7], which include the unique gifts and talents we have to do a particular job in the first instance. We come into the world with nothing[8]; God then gives us the gifts and talents to be successful; which in turn causes us to prosper. It's important to acknowledge and be thankful to Him for equipping us with what we need, so that we can go from a place of having nothing, to making a success of our lives[9].

A Steward is Free from a 'Security Mentality'

Once a person recognizes their role is to manage someone else's property, they're set free from an *ownership* mentality, as well as from the temptation to make money their security. Putting our security in money is a deception that needs to be guarded against. I can point to a one-time event that personally delivered me from this deception, but I find I still need to be aware of the danger so as not to fall back into the trap. The longer we walk with Jesus, the less attractive money becomes and so the less likely we are to fall into the trap it tries to set. Being deceived that money brings happiness is a real danger that can potentially affect *anyone*, so we all need to be vigilant[10].

The antidote to the temptation is to keep looking at Jesus, not our bank balance[11]. Constantly checking a bank or savings account, basing how we feel on what we see points to having taken our eyes off the only One who can bring us true peace and security. The more we look at Jesus, the more we come to know Him and find our purpose in Him. The more we look at Jesus, the less attractive earthly things appear in the light of who He is. The true, eternal, and unshakeable security that we've been created to enjoy can only be found in Him. Earthly things come and go, but God is eternal[12].

A Steward Walks in Humility and Thankfulness

Humility in the area of finances comes from understanding God is willing to trust us with the vast resources He owns[13]. Despite having the potential to get things wrong, God will still trust us to manage His affairs[14]. It amazes me how the God who created the Universe would trust flawed people with His vast resources! When we do get things wrong however, if we're willing to humble ourselves and repent, He is always keen to give us another opportunity.

Experiencing this sort of grace in the world we live in is very rare, but that's how God relates to us every day![15] It's as we walk in the mercy of God that thankfulness begins to become our natural expression. We'll be thankful to Him for trusting us; thankful to Him for providing for us; and thankful for being faithful to His promises. Humility and thankfulness are natural trademarks in the person who recognizes they have the privilege of being called to steward God's resources.

A Steward is Faithful with a Little

Jesus tells us *"Whoever can be trusted with small things can also be trusted with big things. Whoever is dishonest in little things will be dishonest in big things too. If you cannot be trusted with worldly riches, you will not be trusted with the true riches. And if you cannot be trusted with the things that belong to someone else, you will not be given anything of your own. "You cannot serve two masters at the same time. You will hate one master and love the other. Or you will be loyal to one and not care about the other. You cannot serve God and Money at the same time." (Luke 16:10-13 (ERV).*

It's a mistake to think we don't need to be good stewards when we only have a little. How an individual handles a limited amount of money when they're under financial pressure from a number of directions is the litmus test of where their priorities lie. The days of 'small beginnings'[16] is an opportunity nobody can afford to miss, because it's the doorway into greater things. It is the place presented to us to demonstrate what's most important to us - ourselves, or God's Kingdom[17]. If we consistently choose to put God's Kingdom first, we're setting ourselves up for promotion because God knows He can trust us with more.

Notice in these verses how Jesus refers to money as *'worldly'* riches; distinguishing it from what He calls *'true'* riches. The world system defines a rich person by how much money they have. Jesus doesn't. Jesus' definition of a rich person is one who is in possession of 'true' riches. The *true riches* He's referring to are the truths God is willing to reveal to us from His Word when we reverently fear Him and make Him our priority in life[18]. It is these 'true riches' that cause our souls to prosper as we experience the peace, the joy, the security, and the love of God filling us from the inside[19]. A prosperous soul is how the Bible defines a rich person, not what their bank balance says[20]. Money can never bring the lasting fulfilment that the *true riches* from God can. It will try to tell us it can, but we only need to look at how empty some people are, despite their financial wealth, to recognize the false promises money makes.

Stewardship Starts Today

If you feel intimidated by what is involved in being a steward of God's resources, there's no need to be! God doesn't start with the finished product - He starts with the raw materials and then works with them to become fruitful. If you recognize you have been a poor steward up to this point, it doesn't mean you're disqualified. Start by asking God to forgive you for your past mistakes, as well as the foolishness you've shown in the way you've handled money in the past. Then ask Him to help you become the excellent steward you desire to be[21], by teaching you so that you're able to grow into what He has planned for you. By God's grace today can be the first day of your journey. Don't be intimidated by the task, simply pray and ask God to help you, and He will.

The chapters that follow are written to help equip people with some fundamental principles of how to manage their finances so they can become debt-free. These are principles that have worked well for Jill and I on our journey, and so we share them with you from that perspective. They're not exhaustive to the point they cover every situation, because each person is faced with a different set of challenges, as well as a different set of circumstances. Neither are they meant to replace sound counsel with a debt counselling charity or organization. If an individual feels their situation calls for such an approach, don't hesitate to take that route if you need to. We do believe however that applying these principles in the right way will help a great number of people get their finances in order. The principles in and of themselves are not revolutionary, but when they are combined with the spiritual values set out in the earlier part of the book, they will make a difference to an individual's situation, as well as laying a foundation to go beyond debt-freedom into the fulness God has for them.

Wherever you are on your journey, both Jill and I pray that what we've learned over the years will benefit you in ways that goes beyond what we can think or imagine.

24

Knowing the State of Your Flocks

Imagine for a moment you were offered counsel from the world's most prominent authority on financial management - I'm sure you would be eager to hear what they have to say. What's more, they won't charge you a fee - they're happy to give their advice to anyone who wants it. That is effectively what happens when we read what King Solomon writes about financial matters - we're getting free advice from someone who was regarded as the greatest financial expert of his day.

Solomon was financially rich, but he also had a wealth of wisdom. It was his wisdom that helped him become rich in the first instance, as well as then helping him manage the vast wealth he had acquired. He was so renowned in his day that kings and queens sought an audience with him, recognizing the wisdom he was sharing was from God[1]. Solomon is someone who is therefore worthy of our attention when it comes to finances! We can hear what King Solomon had to say simply by reading what he wrote in the Book of Proverbs.

Solomon shared the wisdom of God[2], this is what he had to say:

> [v23] *Learn all you can about your sheep.*
> *Take care of your goats the best you can.*
> [v24] *Neither wealth nor nations last forever.*

v25 *Cut the hay, and new grass will grow.*
Then gather the new plants that grow on the hills.
v26 *Cut the wool from your lambs, and make your clothes.*
Sell some of your goats, and buy some land.
v27 *Then there will be plenty of goat's milk for you and your family,*
with enough to keep the servants healthy.

Proverbs 27:23-27 (ERV)

Sheep, hay, and goats were the common assets people owned at the time Solomon wrote these verses. If we look carefully, there is a direct correlation between how assets were managed, and having enough food (milk) for themselves and their family (v27). Most of us don't depend on crops or livestock to make a living, but if we substitute *'sheep, goats, hay, and land'* for what we have in our possession today, it's possible to learn from the principles Solomon shares in these verses. By applying what he is teaching *to our own personal situation,* we'll end up having plenty to feed ourselves, our family, as well as any others we may have responsibility for (v27). Let's start looking more closely at what Solomon is saying so that we can make it *practically relevant* to our own situation.

STEP 1. 'Learn all you can about your sheep'

Some translations say *"know the state of your flocks",* which means we need to know _everything_ about what we have in our possession. The first thing we need to do from a practical perspective, is to spend time making an inventory of everything related to our financial situation. If we don't know *'the condition of our flocks'* when it comes to finances, trying to become debt-free will be like trying to blow up a balloon when there's a hole in it - no matter how hard we blow, air will continue to escape. Financially, there could be one sizeable expenditure, or a number of smaller ones that may be draining our money without us realizing. Or there may be a gap in the way we manage our budget. Until everything is down on paper in black and white, it's difficult to know where to plug the hole.

If you haven't already done so, it is essential for you to now complete the lists that were suggested in Part 2 of the book. Before continuing, please make sure you have the following lists completed and up to date.

- *'Regular Fixed Payment List'* (see Page 63)

- *'General Spending List'* (see Page 69)

- *'Credit Card & Loan List'* (see Page 75)

Knowing the current state of their finances is the first step that enables the individual to decide where they need to make the necessary adjustments to help them become debt-free.

STEP 2. *'Prayerfully consider what needs to be cut back'*

In the verses Solomon shares with us, he tells us to *"Cut the hay, and new grass will grow" (v25).*

Hay needs to be cut, otherwise it will stop light getting through to the new growth underneath. A new crop can struggle when the hay is left uncut, because the new grass uses its energy to push through, rather than to grow the harvest. The same is true financially when we're looking to become debt-free - we need to look at how we can cut back 'old growth' so that new life can come through unhindered.

The first practical step in cutting back is to look at the *'Regular Fixed Payment List'* to see if there is anything that can be culled immediately. From experience, I know how easy it is to be caught up in the moment by subscribing to something that on reflection, has hardly been used and probably won't be missed when it's gone. Do we still need that film or music streaming subscription? Are we still using the gym membership we were once so enthusiastic about? Now is a good time to look at everything on your list to make sure nothing is draining your resources. As you go through your list, there may be payments that can't be stopped immediately for some reason. Make a note in your calendar as a future reminder so that you don't forget about them. Make sure you look at *everything* - even those things you may find challenging to cut because they've become a 'comfort blanket' to you over the years.

There are no hard and fast rules regarding this process, because everybody's situation is unique. This is why a *prayerful approach* needs to be at the heart of what you do. Through prayer, God will give you the wisdom to know what needs to go, as well as *the faith* to believe that if He's asking you to prune something, it will benefit you. Once you are satisfied you have done as much as you can with your list, add up how much you will start saving and make a note of it.

Now move on to your *'General Spending List'* and do exactly the same thing - prayerfully consider what changes you can make. Is there anything on your list that you're regularly spending money on, but could do without? We obviously need to strike the right balance here, because some will trim back to such an extent that moving towards debt-freedom feels more like an incarceration than a journey! Don't worry if you find things on both your *'Regular Fixed Payment List'*, as well as your *'General Spending List'* that cannot be cut. That's normal and we'll look at what's left in a few moments.

When we approach our lists *prayerfully,* with our hearts open to God, we'll be pleasantly surprised at some of the ways He will help us move forward. Asking God to shine His wisdom on our particular situation prevents the practical aspect of what we're trying to do from becoming a 'dead works'. Seeking Him at every stage brings His life into the process, so the faith and confidence that we're on the right track will grow.

This section is not written to advise people *what* to cut, because everybody's circumstances are different. It is written to emphasize how important it is to know exactly what is happening to our money *("know the state of your flocks")*; as well as encouraging individuals to *personally* seek God on the way forward with regard to what expenditures need to go. The journey towards debt-freedom is unique for every individual, and so by sharing *the principles,* each person can then apply them to their own particular situation and start benefiting from them. If the task of looking at your expenditure seems overwhelming, ask a friend to help you, talk to your Pastor, or contact one of the many debt-counselling organizations that are there to help. The important thing *is to do something,* because doing nothing will keep you where you are, or even worse, take you even further into debt.

25

Tending the Flock

Once you're happy that you've done everything you can with *STEP 2*, it's then time to move on to *STEP 3* and take another look at the items you have remaining on both your *'Regular Fixed Payment'* list, as well as your *'General Spending List'*.

STEP 3. *'Prayerfully consider what can be sheared'*

Solomon tells us to *"Cut the wool from your lambs, and make your clothes" (v26)*. Sheep need looking after, which includes having them sheared. Shearing helps keep the animals healthy because it prevents them from overheating in the summer, as well as reducing infection from flies that bury themselves in the thick fleece. Here again, the principle of what Solomon is teaching can be brought over and applied to our personal financial situation. By 'shearing' the assets we have, we can improve the health of our finances.

What we will find as a result of *STEP 2* is that there will be items on the lists which need to stay. These are normally essential bills and charges that we have a responsibility to pay on a regular basis. The practical aspect of *STEP 3* is to now go back to look at both lists, and bring everything under the microscope of 'can anything be sheared?'

Some items left on the lists are non-negotiable and cannot be sheared, for example taxes set by the local authority linked to property values etc. It is possible however to prune a number of other things that remain on the lists so that expenditure can be further reduced. This will require time and effort, but it is worth doing. Looking for better deals on items such as mobile phone plans, utilities, as well as house and car insurance can be laborious, but is nonetheless necessary so that our finances can return to health. One of the easiest ways to do this is to use a comparison website, but we need to use a reputable one because some earn their commission from the sales, rather than giving the best deals. Reducing the cost of an existing digital TV package by either choosing a different provider, or reducing the actual content of the package is another way of reducing how much we're paying out every month.

When a house or car insurance is due for renewal, don't allow the insurer to automatically renew it as some companies tend to do. Look for a better deal even if it only involves calling the company to ask. If you're armed with a more competitive quote when you contact them, they will be much more likely to bring their price down because they will want to keep your business. As soon as your finances allow, pay for subscriptions and renewals with a one-off annual payment rather than spreading it out with monthly payments that incur interest charges. Make a note of when policies, subscriptions, and plans are due for renewal so you can start looking for a better deal closer to the time. Don't allow things to slip through the net.

We need to do this with both lists - the *'Regular Fixed Payment List'* as well as the *'General Spending List'*. Just like everything we've done so far, a prayerful approach is essential. When we pray and ask God to help us, He will give us the wisdom we need to change things we hadn't even thought of! We'll also find that His favor follows us as we seek Him in what we're doing - this favor shows itself as better deals and refunds etc.

We also need to ask God to give us wisdom to know what we should do with the money we're now saving every month. We need to resist the temptation of simply buying something new for ourselves or our family - a better use is to pay off some of our debt; or use some to sow into someone else's life as a gift; and then treat ourselves or our family if there's any left!

Looking at each individual item and seeing if the cost can be reduced does take time and effort, so it may need to be spread over a number of weeks or months. We need to take the matter seriously however because Solomon tells us to *"Take care of your goats the best you can. Neither wealth nor nations last forever." (v23b - 24).* He's telling us to make every effort to look after what we have, and not to take what we've got for granted! Our responsibility as good stewards is to be patient and diligent in turning things around. When we take this approach, debt-freedom will become a reality in our lives, even if it doesn't happen as quickly as we would like it to.

Once you are happy you've adjusted your lists as far as you're able to, keep on top of things and make a note of how much you have been able to further reduce your expenditure by.

STEP 4. 'Prayerfully consider what you can sell'

Now that you've sheared the *'Regular Fixed Payment'* and *'General Spending List'* to the best of your ability, you're ready to proceed with what Solomon advises next - *"Sell some of your goats, and buy some land" (v26b).* Selling part of what they owned gave them the necessary funds to buy land on which they could build their homes.

What have you got in your possession that you could sell? Over the years, all of us have accumulated 'stuff'; things that we no longer use and have ended up in the attic space, the shed, or somewhere in the garage. The practical element of **STEP 4** is to look at what we've got that is no longer of use to us, and then do something with it. Put some time aside to go through items you've bought over the years but are no longer using, then decide whether you still need it, or whether it can go. As long as it's yours to dispose of, do *something* with it! One approach to this practical exercise is to split it into three lots - things you want to give away or donate; things you're planning on selling; and things you need to recycle or take to the dump. If nothing else, this exercise will give you a feel-good factor because you'll be doing something you've been planning on doing for years, but until now haven't got round to it!

There are plenty of places where we can give stuff away for free - charity shops, family, friends and work colleagues. We need to be careful *what* we give away though. If we see this as an exercise to get rid of the trash we have collected, we're doing ourselves more harm than good by giving it to someone else. Remember that *whatever* a man sows, is what he reaps[1]. If we're sowing broken, close to useless stuff into other people's lives, this is what we can expect in return. Think about whether the recipient is going to appreciate what you're giving them, or is it obvious you're just trying to get rid of what you regard as useless? Don't try to make it look like a 'gift' - explain what you are doing and how you were just wondering whether they would appreciate it or not.

What we give to people reflects the value we place on them as individuals. This is true in the context of this practical exercise, as much as it is when we're genuinely giving someone a gift. Giving a second-hand, unwanted item as a 'gift' is deceiving people on many different levels, and it can be very damaging to a relationship if the recipient finds out. Make sure therefore that your friendship isn't damaged by your enthusiasm to clear stuff out! With the items we're looking at selling, the various options available to do this are huge, so we're not exploring them here.

As we consider the advice Solomon gives in the verses we've been looking at, the direct result of *knowing their flock*[v23]; *cutting the hay*[v25]; *shearing the sheep*[v26]; and *selling some goats*[v26] is that the people could look forward to *a new harvest (new grass)*[v25]; *wool for clothes*[v26]; *money to buy land*[v26]; as well as *food for their family ('milk')*[v27].

As we ourselves look to follow **STEPS 1- 4** which are based on Solomon's wisdom, we are effectively applying his instruction into our own personal situation. Because God's wisdom through Solomon is timeless, we too can expect to experience the same results - to see *new growth* coming; to have *clothes to wear*; to be able to *buy land to have our homes on*; as well as to have *plenty of food to feed our family*, (and any others we may have responsibility for). If I was the one making these promises to you, then you would have no reason to put your hope in them. But because it is God who has given us this wisdom in His Word, we have every reason to be hopeful that when we ask Him to help us walk into the joy of financial freedom, He will[2].

26

Dealing with Interest Payments

You now need to turn your attention to the *'Credit Card & Loan List'* which you brought together earlier (see Page 75). As a reminder, this is a list of every credit card and other outstanding loan you have that is incurring an interest charge. Once you've checked the individual interest rates on each credit card or loan, arrange them in descending order, with the one with the highest interest rate at the top.

STEP 5. *'Attack Your Interest Payments'*

Banks and credit agencies provide a service of lending money to people, making their profit by charging interest. When interest charges are applied, the value of the item being bought is the same; it is the interest being charged to borrow the money that makes it more expensive. Whether the interest is applied at the point of purchase, or later on a credit card statement makes no difference - one way or another borrowing money means the individual is paying more than the item is worth. Becoming debt-free means we get to a place financially where there is no need for us to pay a bank or credit agency, because we no longer require the service they offer when we're making a purchase.

A credit card has its advantages. It is convenient and easy to use especially when ordering online, as well as offering an element of insurance on some purchases. But as soon as it takes us to a place where we are paying interest on what we're buying, it becomes an enemy. It starts off by making itself out to be a friend, offering itself as the gateway to buying the things we desire, but we're not willing to wait for them. But then it brings the sting in its tail, because it takes the individual into the bondage of interest payments. For this reason, anyone who is paying interest on a credit card or loan needs to see that credit card or loan as an enemy. Once we see it as an enemy, we'll stand up to it and fight it so we can bring it down.

There needs to be a plan in place for getting rid of debt. If you are in so much debt that you feel you are sinking, it is time for you to get advice from someone who can come alongside you and help formulate a plan on your behalf. Some debt-counselling agencies have the ability to negotiate with creditors for a pause or reduction in interest payments to give the one in debt some time to bring a repayment plan together. If that's you, seek help by contacting your Pastor initially, who will then be able to point you in the right direction.

Those individuals who may not be in a desperate place, but still feel the need to take positive steps towards getting rid of their debt, also need a plan! The essence of the plan is very simple. From your list, start by targeting the credit card / loan that has the highest interest rate - the one at the top of your list. Without neglecting the others, start paying as much as you can above the required amount on this credit card (or loan). When you get an unexpected payment or bonus from somewhere, take at least part of it and use it to pay off more of what you owe, carrying this on until the debt on this first credit card is totally cleared. Take an aggressive approach to the extent that once the balance is zero, get rid of the card by cutting it into pieces, then contact the credit company to cancel it.

Then move onto the next credit card / loan on your list. Do the same again, aggressively attacking it by paying over and above what is required, using any spare money you have, until this one is cleared as well. If the amount owed is similar to the first one, what you will see happening is that you're able to clear this one quicker! To start with, the interest charges are not as high as the previous one. You won't be incurring interest charges on the previous credit card either because you've just got rid of it, which leaves you more money to target this next one on your list. Once the whole balance has been cleared, get rid of this credit card as well! Carry this on until you only have only one credit card left, and the balance on it is zero.

Now you are in a position where you need to make a choice. Are you going to use this last credit card as a convenient friend, making sure any outstanding amount is paid off before interest charges are applied? Or are you going to allow it to bring you back into the bondage of interest payments that you've just been delivered from? The choice is down to how disciplined you feel you can be, but if you're in any doubt that you may slip back into old habits, get rid of this one as well and start looking at other ways of paying for the things you buy.

This method of clearing credit card (or loan) debts is a very effective one because as you go down your list it generates an avalanche effect - gathering pace as it travels. As with all the practical steps we've looked at, a prayerful approach is essential with this one as well. Ask God to give you the 'fight' you need to get rid of your debt, as well as a fire in your belly so that you don't quit half-way.

Tackling a Mortgage

A mortgage on a house or business is often the biggest debt an individual owes, so the prospect of clearing it may appear daunting. Here are some pointers regarding how to specifically approach clearing a mortgage, or any other large debt you're looking to get rid of.

[1.] *Add faith into the mix.* There is a *natural* way of clearing a mortgage, which is to keep up with the repayments over the course of the agreement, so that the debt is eventually repaid. This can take up to twenty or thirty years, depending on the terms of the contract. But the approach we want to take is to clear the mortgage *supernaturally*, which means we're not prepared to simply wait for the natural process to run its course. Obviously, it's important to keep up the regular repayments, but at the same time another 'ingredient' needs to be added into the mix - faith in God and His ability to do something beyond what we can do naturally. To clear a mortgage with God, we're not to limit ourselves to the practical steps alone, but to also exercise faith in His promises. It is faith *and* practical steps that will enable us to clear a mortgage early with God. Adding faith into the mix comes by continually reminding ourselves of what God has promised in His Word[1].

[2.] *Fully commit to God's will for your life.* Looking to God to help us become debt-free, but then walking a path independent of Him once we've found our financial freedom will lead to disaster. Having more disposable income as a result of not having debt gives the individual more money to indulge their flesh. The story of the Prodigal Son is not only a parable about the forgiving love of God as a Father; it is also a warning of the destructive effects a material inheritance can have on the individual who chooses to turn their back on their relationship with God[2]. We need to therefore be fully committed to our relationship with God first and foremost, seeking His Kingdom and will for our lives as a priority[3].

[3.] *Get rid of unbelief.* Having a mortgage is a normal and accepted mind-set in the world system, and it's one that most of us will have grown up with and have become accustomed to. In the Kingdom of God however, debt of any description is not normal. This is clear from God's promise that His people will lend to many nations, but not borrow[4]. We're also told by the apostle Paul to owe no man anything except to love them[5]. There is no 'small print' with these promises telling us that a mortgage is the exception. Being debt-free includes being free from a mortgage, no matter how daunting that may appear to us at the outset. In order that a Kingdom of God mindset becomes natural to us, we need to meditate on God's promises regarding finances. Meditating on God's promises replaces the thoughts that try to oppose what God has for us, with the truth of what He has said in His Word[6].

[4.] *Do what you can in the natural.* We're probably familiar with the quote *"How do you eat an elephant? The answer - one bite at a time!"*. The point is this, when we're faced with a task that looks overwhelming, we need to approach it in small chunks. With a mortgage or other large debt, we need to do what we can, even when what we're doing seems relatively small and insignificant. If our hearts are positioned in faith towards God, He will add His supernatural to our natural, even when our natural is small[7]. In practice, the minimum we should do is continue to be faithful to the commitment we've made to the lender regarding repayments. But as and when we can, we should start to pay more than what we're required to pay, so that we're eating away at more of the elephant every month. As we do that, there will be less of it left! As God then adds His supernatural to our natural, at some point we'll begin to notice the process accelerating.

5. *Take a patient approach.* Trying to eat an elephant too quickly would lead to indigestion, and if 'elephant' was the only thing on the menu every day, we would soon get tired of it. Everybody needs a balanced, healthy diet in their lives. We need to make sure therefore that not all of our focus is on clearing the mortgage, especially to the extent we start to neglect other aspects of God's financial system (both spiritual and practical). Even if the mortgage is our biggest challenge, we're not to allow it to be our biggest priority. Seeking God's Kingdom and His righteousness should always be first in our lives, because as we do that, all the other things will be given to us as well[8].

6. *Seek professional advice regarding whether the borrowing agreement you have is the best one for you.* Personal circumstances, as well as mortgage agreements (terms of lending) are continually changing in line with what is happening in the global financial markets. In our enthusiasm to get our first mortgage, and possibly our inexperience in looking for the best deal, we may not be on the best borrowing terms available to us. Seek some professional advice therefore to see if the interest rates you are paying can be reduced. Mortgages are a specialist field so there is a need to tread carefully in this area by seeking sound, independent advice.

27

Budgeting Made Easy

When someone has a budget, it means they have a plan for how they propose to use the money they have in their possession. Having a budget empowers the individual to take control of their money. It means they will be able to regulate their spending; plan ahead for unexpected costs; and formulate a plan for getting rid of their debt. The opposite is true for someone who does not have a budget in place - they are more likely to overspend and add to their debt, especially when unexpected bills arrive.

A random or haphazard approach to finances puts people in a place of vulnerability, because financial pressures have the potential to cause an increase in issues such as stress and depression[1]. Relationships can also be a casualty of poor money management. Friends, families, and even marriages can fall apart as a result of financial pressures. A budget therefore not only helps bring *financial* health and freedom, it also has the knock-on effect of benefiting the *general wellbeing* of an individual, as well as the relationships they have.

There are many different ways to manage, or to budget an income. In this chapter we'll look at the simple budget plan Jill and I have used for nearly two decades. In conjunction with the other keys already covered, this plan has helped us become debt-free in the first instance, and then remain debt-free even though we've experienced some lean times during that period.

Which budget plan you choose is not the most important thing. What counts is that you have *some sort* of plan in place to manage your finances, because without a plan it will be extremely difficult to experience the debt-freedom you desire, and then to remain debt-free once you've achieved it.

A Simple Way of Budgeting

Imagine you have an apple pie in front of you that needs to be shared between four people. Not all the pieces will be the same size because people's appetites are different. This is a simple way of looking at our budget plan - the income coming in each month is the pie; which then needs to be cut into four different sized pieces.

The first thing we need to do is check how big the pie is, so start off by writing down exactly what your total income is for the period you're budgeting (usually monthly). Once you know the size of the pie, you can then start cutting into it. There are four main parts that need to be budgeted for, which are set out below in order of priority.

1. Tithe

2. Bills and Regular Expenditures

3. Savings

4. Personal Spending

1. Tithe

The tithe is always ten percent, so we can work this out once we know our total income. We've already seen earlier in the book how giving the first ten percent is honoring to God, so we need to deal with the tithe before anything else[2]. Once we've worked out the amount, I personally believe there is value in 'sending' it to its destination before looking at the remaining ninety percent.

2. Bills and Regular Expenditures

We all have a responsibility to pay our bills, so we need to make sure we meet this obligation before spending money on ourselves. Not having enough money to pay our bills leads to further debt and additional interest charges. It is essential therefore to budget in a way that allows us to first of all meet the responsibilities we have to pay those who are providing us with a service.

Make a list of every bill that needs to be paid. Try to anticipate other regular expenditures as well - things like gasoline, food, pocket money etc. Knowing we have the money set aside to pay for the things we know will be coming up takes a lot of pressure off us financially. Also include here the money you need to pay off credit cards or loans, as well as any mortgage or rent. The previous lists you've been working on should help you identify most of the things that need to go in this second part of the budget. (*'Regular Fixed Payment List'* / *'General Spending List'* / *'Credit Card & Loan List'*)

3. Savings

If you're not already putting money aside for savings, now is a good time to start, even if the amount you're able to afford initially is very small. Saving just a small amount establishes the principle of not spending everything you have. As it builds up, this money can then be used to help meet unexpected bills, as well as planning for a vacation etc.

4. Personal Spending

Having sent our tithe; paid all our bills and debt obligations; put some money aside for savings; we're now in a position to know how much we can spend on ourselves. Often people buy things not knowing whether they can afford them or not, and so end up worrying what will happen when their bank or credit card statement arrives. This takes a lot of the joy out of buying an item, and can often leave the individual feeling guilty. All of this is removed as a result of budgeting and knowing exactly what money there is left over for 'personal spend'.

If you're not used to budgeting your income, the amount you're left with for personal use may look disappointing because you are used to more. This is normal, as one of the main reasons people are in debt is because their spending exceeds their income. Budgeting sets out in black and white exactly how much there is left for personal spending, and so takes the 'guesswork' out of whether you can afford something or not. It is from this portion of the budget that you should also be looking to sow into other people's lives (see Chapter 18).

A good motivator for working on finding better deals on your regular bills etc. is to realize that the savings you make there, will end up in this 'personal spending' bracket. Don't be tempted to spend it all on yourself however - a better use of what you save by 'shearing' your bills can be used to pay off more of your debt so that financial freedom comes earlier.

It is _essential_ to put boundaries on this personal spending part of the budget, otherwise there will be little, or even no progress towards becoming debt-free. The person who hopes to become debt-free without changing the way they spend money is fooling themselves. Something has to change, and staying within the boundary of what you have left is a vital part of reaching the goal of financial freedom.

Limiting ourselves to what we have in this _Personal Spending_ part of the budget requires discipline, and God will help us with this if we ask Him. A lack of self-discipline contributes to increased debt, but in Christ, God has gone ahead of us and given us His Holy Spirit to turn things around for us. That's because one of the fruits of the Spirit is _self-discipline_[3]. Will-power and self-sacrifice are not a permanent solution to dealing with finances, or any other area in our lives where we need to see a lasting change. To experience the transformation we're looking for, we need to have our _hearts_ changed. God will change us at a heart level if we truly want that change, and ask Him to help us. As the Holy Spirit helps us stay within the boundaries of what we have, the discipline we develop during this stage of our journey will stay with us. As we leave debt behind, and begin to walk in abundance, God is able to trust us with more of His resources because He knows we have the discipline to handle them well.

A budget plan enables the individual to take control of their finances because it tells them exactly _where_ they're spending their money, and _on what. With that information comes the ability_ *to make right choices.* Some of the choices are difficult to make, because it means saying 'no' to certain things which normally they would not hesitate to buy. A budget plan brings the individual to the place where *they now control their finances,* rather than *their finances controlling them.* With God's guidance and wisdom, it is possible to navigate a way out of debt, and walk into the joy of financial freedom that awaits. Having a budget plan is an essential part of realizing that dream.

28

Multiple Streams of Income

In looking at the practical aspects of becoming debt-free, the main focus has been on *expenditure* - how to deal with the money we have in our possession. But there is another important aspect to managing finances as well, which is *income*. Both income and expenditure go hand in hand; they are two sides of the same financial coin. The more income we're able to generate, the more we're able to give as a tithe; the easier it is to pay our bills; the quicker we'll get rid of our debt; and the more we have to spend on ourselves and to help others. Everyone is a winner when income increases! In this last chapter it is important therefore to look at how *income* fits in with God's bigger plan for the follower of Christ.

God Desires Increase

The first thing we need to get clear in our minds, as well as established in our hearts is that God does not want His children to struggle financially. In fact, the opposite is true, because God's plan for His family is for them to thrive and be successful[1]. During times of financial struggle, we need to keep the truth of God's Word before us so that we're not deceived into thinking financial lack is His will. When financial challenges come, we should use them as opportunities to believe what God has promised, and then by faith take the land of plenty He wants us to possess[2]. The simple truth is that financial lack is out to destroy us[3], whereas God wants to prosper us[4].

Jesus came to reveal the nature of God as a loving Father. Earthly fathers who love their children want the best for them. They want to see them excel in every area of life - sport, academia, or a chosen career. Unfortunately, many people don't see God in this way, but see Him as mean and demanding, even putting obstacles in people's way to make life harder. This is not what Jesus revealed about God the Father. Jesus tells us that God is a better Father than any earthly father could ever be[5]. So, whenever we witness how wonderfully a loving, earthly father relates to his child, we need to 'supersize' it to understand what God is like! We cannot *learn* the truth that God is a caring Father - it has to be *revealed* to us. The revelation comes through a relationship with God in Jesus Christ, where we come to know by *experience* what God is really like[6]. This does not come because we've read about it, or somebody else has told us, but because we've had a *personal* encounter with the love of God in Christ. Once we experience the reality of who God is, we will never be the same again.

We need to make sure that what we believe about God is aligned with the truth of what Jesus revealed. We should not allow past experience, wrong teaching, or disappointments to shape how we view God, because this keeps us from experiencing the true nature of God, which is love[7]. If we believe something about God that is contrary to what Jesus revealed in His earthly ministry, then we need to question what we believe. To get a revelation of the true nature of God, we need to read about Jesus in the Gospels[8], and as we do, ask the Holy Spirit to reveal God's nature to us[9] by pouring His love in our hearts so that we *experience* this truth[10].

The *truth* about God as a Father is that He wants His children to flourish[11]. The *truth* about God as a Father is that He delights and takes pleasure in seeing His children thrive[12]. The *truth* about God as Father is that He wants to share everything He has with His children[13]. An earthly father's desire to see their child experience success is fashioned after the One who created the heart within them. As we go on to look at the income side of things, it needs to be in the light of the revelation of the truth that God wants His children to prosper!

There is Gold Inside Every Believer

God is the Creator who created man *in His own image*[14]. This image was lost at the Fall, but is restored through faith in Christ[15]. What this means is that the *creative nature* of God dwells within every Christian who is born of the Spirit[16]. There are many ways by which this creative nature is released through an individual's life - one of them is through innovative ideas and strategies. God is eager to share His wisdom with His children[17], giving them ideas that will not only provide an income, but will also benefit society as a whole.

Think of it like gold that is waiting to be discovered. It's possible for the gifts, talents, and creative ideas that God has given to remain dormant, with the individual not even being aware they are there. We have to sometimes dig for this gold, so that gifts can be realized and then used to come up with creative ideas that can be taken forward and developed. Doing this brings *personal* benefit, because it gives the individual a sense of achievement, excitement, and fulfilment. God's panorama however is not just for the individual, because using gifts and talents in the right way blesses others as well, and brings glory to God.

Thinking Outside the Box

The apostle John shares the account of how Jesus showed Himself to a number of the disciples by the Sea of Galilee after the resurrection. The disciples had been fishing all night, but had caught nothing[18]. As dawn broke, Jesus was standing on the shoreline. Knowing they hadn't caught anything, He said to them *"Cast the net on the right-hand side of the boat and you will find a catch"*. They followed His instruction, and ended up with such a large catch of fish that they struggled to haul it in[19].

This was a challenging time for the disciples. They had been following Jesus for three years believing He was the promised Messiah, but were helpless as they watched Him being crucified. Even though Jesus had already appeared to some of them after His resurrection, they were still confused about what they should be doing next. (Jesus hadn't yet commissioned them to take the Gospel to others). The only way they knew how to make a living was fishing, so they went back to what was familiar. It was in the midst of their confusion that Jesus appeared to them once more, and gave them the *specific instruction* to cast their net on the right side of the boat. Some of them were experienced fishermen, but it wasn't until Jesus gave them this instruction that they started to catch anything. Once they did what He said, they caught such a huge catch that it took all of them to bring it to the shore.

Jesus, by His Holy Spirit, is still giving instructions today on how to land a huge catch. We can look at this account in the light of 'catching men'[20], but we can also learn from it as we apply it to other areas of our lives as we follow Jesus. This is what happened to Jill and I in 2008. After a number of failed attempts at trying to get a job, we were in a low place, with no idea what we should do next. We were living on the bare minimum as far as income was concerned and nothing was opening up despite our best efforts. Then the Holy Spirit spoke to us through this account.

I had been looking for work through traditional, familiar routes which involved looking for an employer who would hire me. As I read this account of the disciples, God spoke to my heart to *cast my net on the right side of the boat*, effectively saying I needed to do things differently. I needed to start thinking 'outside the box'. It took a while for us to understand what casting the net on the right side of the boat meant for us personally, but once it became clear, we took the step and have never looked back. What God spoke to us through this passage brought a radical change in the way we generate income, and we're still benefiting from a new way of thinking even today.

What About You?

Is Jesus asking you to think 'outside the box' with regard to how you can bring in an income? You may be doing things the only way you know how to, and like the disciples may have lots of experience doing it, but it seems you're making little progress. Can I encourage you to take some time to read this passage of Scripture[21] and then open your heart to the Holy Spirit, asking Him to speak to you *personally*.

Pray specifically that God would give you new, innovative ideas that will help you increase your income. Give Him the opportunity to help you look at things from a different perspective, as well as giving you the clarity to know what 'different' could look like in your situation. There are many Christians who are more qualified than I am to teach about how God gives innovative ideas to people. Having introduced the subject, I would encourage you to explore this area for yourself and learn from others who have a great deal of experience in this area.

It is important to be thankful to God for the job that brings us a regular, steady income. But we need to make sure we don't settle to the extent we miss something bigger God may have for us. Ask God to show you the various things you could do in addition to your 'normal' job. There are occasions where we may need to work extra hours for financial reasons, but working long hours and having a number of different jobs to make ends meet is not God's best for us. God's long-term plan is for us not to become exhausted and burnt out as a result of over-working. His plan is for us to have a *balanced* life, where we get to enjoy every aspect of it - including work. He wants to remove the yoke of having to work so hard that we miss out on spending time with our family as well as having time to relax.

As God gives you creative ideas and inventions, look to generate a number of different streams of income, from a number of different directions. Not being dependent on one source of income allows the follower of Jesus to be flexible and able to respond more easily to God's call when a change of direction is required. It also means that if one source of income starts to dry up, the others are there to help sustain during dry seasons.

What Does Your Heart Tell You?

Hopefully this chapter will have stirred a passion within you to think more about God's bigger picture for your life with regard to your income. Make a list of the gifts you have, as well as the desires you carry in your heart. What are you good at? What dreams do you have that you would like to fulfill? What do you enjoy doing? Write everything down on paper and keep it before you as you pray for direction[22]. Ask God to take away the dreams and desires that are not from Him, and to strengthen the ones that are. Over a period of time some of the things you once desired will become less important, while others will become a priority. Again, remember that the gifts, talents, and creative ideas God gives you are not just for your benefit. There is a bigger picture with God, and as we walk in the plan God has for *us*, others benefit as well, and He is glorified.

A quote by Howard Thurman that has stayed with me for a number of years is this: *"Don't ask yourself what the world needs. Ask yourself what makes you come alive, and go do that, because what the world needs is people who have come alive"*. As we find the things that make us come alive, the promise of Almighty God is that *"He will make you successful in everything you do"*[23].

Both Jill and I pray that this book will strengthen you as you journey towards financial freedom with God. Before we bring things to a close, there is one final practical exercise that needs to be done. Having gone through the book and engaged with the practical aspects that have been recommended, write down five words that best describe how you feel <u>now</u> about your financial situation. Are you hopeful? Are you encouraged? Once you have a list of five words, refer back to the five words you wrote down *at the start* of your journey, and compare them (see Page 15). Even if it is only the attitude of your heart that has changed at this stage, and that you're still waiting for your finances to turn around, start thanking God for the hope, as well as the promises He has given you, so that you too can experience *The Joy of Financial Freedom!*

"The Lord is good. When people are in trouble, they can go to him for safety. He takes good care of those who trust in him."
(Nahum 1:7 (NIRV)

'Defeating
Fear, Panic,
and Anxiety'

- A 30-day
devotional

Fear, panic, and anxiety are real and debilitating forces that hold people back from reaching their full potential in life. Jesus came to set us free from these bondages so that we could experience life as God intended it to be. This 30-day devotional looks at what Christ has done to set us free, as well as explaining what the individual's response should be so they can move into the freedom that God promises those who put their faith in Jesus. An essential read for anybody who is struggling with an oppression of any description.

LIVING
OUT OF THE CHRIST WITHIN YOU
A 30-DAY DEVOTIONAL

GWYNEDD JONES

'Living Out of The Christ Within You'

- A 30-day devotional

What it means to be a *'new creation'* in Christ is one of the least taught subjects from the Bible, yet for the Christian it is one of the most important. *'Living Out of The Christ Within You'* is a 30-day devotional that helps bring clarity regarding the spiritual identity of the individual who has put their faith in Jesus Christ. It is as we begin to understand our new identity that we become better equipped to re-present Jesus to the world around us.

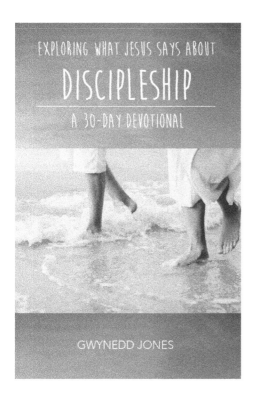

*'Exploring
What Jesus
Says About
Discipleship'*

*- A 30-day
devotional*

Jesus is the best disciple-maker there has ever been, so as followers of Jesus the least we can do is to hear what He has to say about the subject of discipleship. *'Exploring What Jesus Says About Discipleship'* is a 30-day devotional that looks at some of Jesus' key teachings on discipleship, as well as touching on the principles He used which proved so successful. Whether we see ourselves simply as a follower, or as someone who is discipling others, this book is written to help us hear from the Master Discipler Himself.

'How To Be The Parent-In-Law Your Kids Will Love'

Is your relationship with your child & their spouse (or partner) important to you? Do you want to be relevant as a parent-in-law and add value to their lives? If the answer is *yes* then this book is for you. *'How to be the parent-in-law your kids will love'* looks at some key principles parents need to understand if they are to become excellent parents-in-law; as well as tips on how to avoid some of the common mistakes some parents-in-law make. *'How to be the parent-in-law your kids will love'* is an essential read for every parent who wants to be appreciated and valued by their in-law children, rather than just being tolerated!

Endnotes

(Scriptural references)

Chapter 1

1. John 15:19
2. Colossians 1:13
3. Exodus 22:25; Deuteronomy 15:7-8; 23:19-20; Psalm 112:5
4. Matthew 5:42 (CEV)
5. Isaiah 53:10
6. 1 Corinthians 10:23
7. Deuteronomy 15:6 & 28:12
8. Deuteronomy 28:13
9. Exodus 22:25; Leviticus 25:35-37; Deuteronomy 23:19
10. Deuteronomy 23:20
11. Luke 6:34-36
12. Proverbs 19:17

Chapter 2

1. Proverbs 22:7 (GW) – my emphasis
2. Hebrew - 'ebed – Strong's H5650
3. Hebrew – 'âbad – Strong's H5647
4. Hebrew – lâvâh – Strong's H3867
5. Psalm 37:5
6. Proverbs 21:5 (ERV)
7. Proverbs 22:26-27 (ERV)
8. Psalm 37:21
9. Hebrew – râshâ – Strong's H7563
10. Deuteronomy 15:6; 28:12
11. Deuteronomy 28:43-44 (TLB)
12. Deuteronomy 21:23
13. Galatians 3:13-14
14. Proverbs 10:22; 2 Corinthians 1:20

Chapter 3

1. Genesis 17:1 – (at this stage Abraham was known as Abram)
2. Hebrew – Shadday – Strong's H7706
3. Genesis 12:1 – 25:11
4. Genesis 22:14 – Hebrew – Yehôvâh Yir'eh – Strong's 3070
5. Genesis 22:9-14
6. John 1:29
7. Genesis 17:1
8. Genesis 17:7
9. Galatians 3:7; John 1:12-13

10. 2 Corinthians 1:20
11. Psalm 27:8
12. Matthew 4:4 (CEV)
13. Deuteronomy 8:3
14. John 10:10
15. John 7:37-39
16. Matthew 6:33
17. Matthew 6:32; Luke 12:30
18. Matthew 6:26 (TLB)
19. Matthew 6:28-30; Luke 12:27-28
20. 1 Thessalonians 4:11-12; 2 Thessalonians 3:10-12
21. Matthew 6:33 (AMPC)
22. John 10:10
23. Matthew 7:7-11
24. Matthew 11:27; John 6:46; 7:29; 8:55; 10:15

Chapter 4

1. 1 Samuel 17:42-49
2. 1 Samuel 17:45
3. 2 Corinthians 10:3-5; Philippians 2:9-11
4. 1 Samuel 17:46
5. 1 Samuel 17:47
6. 1 Samuel 17:42-44
7. Exodus 14:14; 1 Samuel 17:47; 2 Chronicles 20:15
8. 1 Samuel 17:1-3
9. Deuteronomy 15:6; 28:12; Romans 13:8
10. Proverbs 3:5-6
11. 1 Corinthians 2:14
12. Galatians 5:17
13. 1 Timothy 6:12
14. Deuteronomy 30:19-20
15. 2 Corinthians 5:7
16. Proverbs 4:25 (NLT)
17. 1 Samuel 17:49
18. James 1:5-6
19. Isaiah 55:9
20. Amos 4:13; 1 Corinthians 2:9-13
21. Proverbs 1:7; 10:21; 18:2; 23:9; 24:7; 28:26
22. Proverbs 3:13-15; 4:7-9; 16:16
23. Proverbs 8:1-11; 9:1-6
24. 1 Kings 19:12 (KJV)

Chapter 5

1. Mark 10:17
2. Mark 10:22; Luke 18:23
3. Luke 18:18 - the Greek word for 'ruler' used by Luke is *'archōn'* (Strong's G758 – which means 'ruler / prince / chief / magistrate')
4. Mark 10:19-20; Luke 18:20-21
5. Mark 10:17; Luke 18:18
6. Mark 10:22
7. Mark 10:17; Luke 18:18
8. Mark 10:19-20; Luke 18:20-21
9. Romans 6:23; Ephesians 2:8
10. Exodus 20:3; Deuteronomy 5:7
11. Mark 10:21; Luke 18:22
12. Mark 10:21
13. Matthew 6:24 (NIRV)
14. Matthew 6:33 (ERV)
15. Matthew 6:24-33
16. Matthew 6:24
17. Matthew 6:25-32
18. Matthew 6:33
19. Proverbs 23:4-5
20. Ecclesiastes 5:10 (CEV)
21. Matthew 6:21 (CEV)
22. John 10:10 (AMPC)
23. Galatians 2:21
24. Mark 4:19; Luke 8:14
25. Mark 8:36
26. Hebrews 13:5
27. Matthew 13:45-46
28. Matthew 25:14-30
29. Matthew 25:24
30. Matthew 25:25
31. Matthew 25:21 & 23
32. Psalm 67:1-2
33. 1 Timothy 6:10 (AMPC)
34. 1 John 1:9
35. James 4:6-10; 1 Peter 5:6
36. Romans 10:10
37. John 16:13
38. John 15:26

Chapter 6

1. Romans 12:2; Ephesians 4:22-24
2. Romans 12:2 (NIRV)
3. Luke 6:40
4. Matthew 25:20-23
5. Luke 16:11 (ERV)
6. Acts 10:34; Romans 2:11
7. Matthew 25:15
8. Matthew 25:19-20
9. Matthew 25:20-21
10. Acts 20:35 (GW - emphasis added).
11. Ephesians 5:1
12. Deuteronomy 15:10-11; Proverbs 19:17.
13. Proverbs 3:27-28; Matthew 10:8
14. Genesis 12:2
15. Matthew 25:21
16. Luke 21:1-4
17. 1 Peter 5:6-7
18. John 17:17

Chapter 7

1. Romans 5:12
2. Jeremiah 17:9 (NIRV)
3. Romans 7:18 (GW)
4. Psalm 11:7; 119:137; 129:4; 145:17 as examples
5. Isaiah 40:12-14
6. Proverbs 9:1-6; James 3:17
7. Genesis 26:1, 12-14
8. Deuteronomy 28:12; Joshua 21:45
9. John 8:34; Romans 6:16
10. Galatians 5:19-21
11. Matthew 7:13
12. Credit Suisse Global Wealth Report 2020
13. Psalm 12:5; 35:10; 41:1-2; Proverbs 19:17; 29:7; 31:9 as examples
14. Proverbs 22:16 (NLT)
15. Ezekiel 36:26-27
16. 2 Corinthians 5:17
17. John 3:3
18. Ephesians 4:24; 5:1
19. Matthew 5:48
20. John 15:19; 17:14-19
21. 2 Corinthians 8:20-21

Chapter 8

1. Isaiah 55:8-9 (NLT)
2. Romans 12:2
3. Ephesians 4:22-24
4. Romans 8:7
5. 1 Corinthians 2:14
6. Matthew 5:48; Ephesians 5:1
7. 1 Corinthians 2:16
8. Ephesians 1:3
9. Amos 4:13; 1 Corinthians 2:9-13
10. Ephesians 3:20; Matthew 17:20 (KJV)
11. Matthew 14:22-33
12. Romans 8:5-8
13. 2 Corinthians 10:4-5

Chapter 9

1. The Biblical term for this is *'renewal of the mind'* - Romans 12:2
2. 2 Corinthians 8:11-13
3. Luke 6:38 (NLT)
4. Luke 6:36
5. Proverbs 11:24-25 (TLB)
6. Matthew 14:29
7. Romans 12:3
8. James 2:17
9. Proverbs 3:5

Chapter 10

1. Leviticus 19:35-36; Ezekiel 45:10
2. Proverbs 11:1; 20:10; 20:23
3. Hosea 12:6-7; Micah 6:10-13
4. Mark 12:17 (WE)
5. Romans 13:1-3 (WE)
6. Ecclesiastes 5:12
7. Genesis 23:1-20
8. Acts 13:22
9. 2 Samuel 24:18-25
10. Philippians 2:3 (ERV)
11. Romans 5:12
12. Genesis 2:7
13. Genesis 1:29-30

14. 1 Peter 1:23
15. 2 Corinthians 5:17
16. John 3:3 *(some translations use 'born-again' / 'born-anew')*
17. Matthew 7:7-11
18. Genesis 22:14 – Hebrew – *Yehôvâh Yir'eh* – Strong's 3070
19. Matthew 6:33
20. Romans 5:17
21. Psalm 119:105; Proverbs 4:26-27
22. Matthew 5:13-16
23. Matthew 5:10
24. Romans 14:17
25. Isaiah 53:5; John 14:27
26. Psalm 23:6

Chapter 11

1. Ephesians 4:28 - emphasis mine
2. 1 Timothy 5:8
3. Ephesians 5:1
4. Deuteronomy 28:9-10; Psalm 67:1-2
5. Jeremiah 31:33; Ezekiel 36:26-27
6. Acts 20:35
7. Acts 10:34
8. Titus 2:11
9. Deuteronomy 30:19
10. Romans 6:16
11. Hebrews 11:6

Chapter 12

1. Deuteronomy 30:19-20
2. James 2:14-17
3. Psalm 25:14; Jeremiah 33:3
4. Philippians 4:19
5. 2 Corinthians 3:18; Ephesians 4:24
6. Matthew 6:33
7. Proverbs 8:17-21

Chapter 13

1. John 2:1-11
2. Matthew 8:23-27; Mark 4:35-41; Luke 8:22-25
3. Matthew 21:18-22; Mark 11:12-14, 20-25
4. Nehemiah 6:15-16
5. Amos 9:13
6. Amos 9:13 (MSG).
7. Hebrews 13:8
8. James 2:17
9. Psalm 37:4
10. Isaiah 55:1-3
11. Hebrews 4:2 (TLB) - my emphasis

Chapter 14

1. John 4:24
2. Matthew 6:8
3. John 11:41-42
4. Matthew 7:7-8 - my emphasis
5. Isaiah 40:8
6. John 1:18; 6:46
7. Matthew 5:48
8. Matthew 7:9-11
9. Luke 12:32
10. John 11:41-42
11. John 3:16
12. Jeremiah 31:34; John 17:3
13. Mark 11:24 (NIRV)
14. 1 John 5:14-15
15. Matthew 6:7 (TLB)
16. Matthew 6:8; Daniel 9:18-23 (especially v. 23); Daniel 10:12
17. Mark 11:24
18. Luke 18:1-8
19. Luke 18:7-8
20. Luke 18:8
21. Psalm 37:4
22. Jeremiah 29:11-13

Chapter 15

1. 1 Corinthians 13:3; 2 Corinthians 9:7
2. Genesis 4:1-5
3. Genesis 4:3-4 (NIRV)
4. Proverbs 3:9-10 (TLB)
5. James 2:17
6. Psalm 35:27

Chapter 16

1. Numbers 18:1-7
2. Numbers 18:23-24; Deuteronomy 18:1; Joshua 13:14; 13:33; 14:4; 18:7
3. Numbers 18:21, 24
4. Numbers 18:26; Nehemiah 10:38
5. Deuteronomy 14:28-29
6. Hebrews 8:1-5; 10:1
7. Hebrews 3:1; 4:14-16; 7:26-28; 8:1; 9:11
8. Genesis 14:18; Hebrews 5:5-6; 5:9-10; 6:19-20
9. Genesis 14:12-20
10. Genesis 14:17-20
11. Numbers 18:8
12. Malachi 3:10
13. 1 Corinthians 9:13-14

Chapter 17

1. 1 Corinthians 2:14
2. Romans 8:7-8; Galatians 5:17
3. Deuteronomy 14:28-29
4. Proverbs 3:9-10
5. Proverbs 11:24 (ERV)
6. 2 Chronicles 9:22
7. 2 Chronicles 1:7-12
8. 2 Chronicles 1:12
9. Malachi 3:10
10. Malachi 3:9
11. Galatians 3:13
12. Deuteronomy 30:19-20
13. James 2:17
14. Matthew 6:33
15. John 14:15
16. Mark 10:23; Luke 18:24

216

17. John 4:24
18. Luke 18:27 (NLT)
19. John 8:36; Romans 5:20; Hebrews 4:16
20. John 10:10

Chapter 18

1. Matthew 6:21 (NLT)
2. Matthew 6:33; John 10:10
3. Galatians 5:1-6
4. 2 Corinthians 9:7 (NLT) - emphasis added
5. Strong's G2431
6. Mark 12:41-44
7. Exodus 25:2 (ERV) - emphasis added
8. Leviticus 27:30; Deuteronomy 14:22
9. John 1:17; Romans 6:14
10. Ephesians 1:6, 2:8-9
11. Titus 2:11-12
12. Deuteronomy 10:16; Jeremiah 4:4; Romans 2:28-29
13. Jeremiah 31:33; Ezekiel 36:26-27; 2 Corinthians 5:17
14. Matthew 5:44
15. Matthew 5:38-42
16. Matthew 5:20, 48
17. 2 Chronicles 16:9
18. Hebrews 11:6
19. Figures from the US show how families who have an income of less than $20K per year are *eight times more likely* to tithe than families who have an income greater than $75K per year. (*https://www.sharefaith.com/blog/2015/12/facts-christians-tithing/*)

Chapter 19

1. 1 Timothy 6:17-18; Hebrews 13:16; 1 John 3:17
2. Matthew 11:28-30
3. Psalm 139:23
4. Acts 20:35
5. Ephesians 5:1; 1 John 3:1-23; 4:7, 11, 20-21
6. 1 Corinthians 12:5; Romans 12:6-8
7. 2 Corinthians 9:12-15
8. 1 Corinthians 3:9
9. Genesis 8:22; Galatians 6:7
10. Luke 6:37-38

11. Genesis 8:22
12. Proverbs 11:24; 1 John 3:17-18
13. Mark 4:20
14. 2 Corinthians 9:6 (NIRV)
15. 2 Corinthians 8:13 (GW)
16. 2 Corinthians 8:12
17. 1 Timothy 5:8
18. 2 Corinthians 9:10-11
19. Matthew 6:21
20. Matthew 6:33
21. 2 Chronicles 16:9a
22. Acts 20:35
23. Genesis 1:11-12 (TLB)
24. Luke 6:37-38
25. Galatians 6:7 (NIRV)
26. Genesis 1:29; Isaiah 28:23-29
27. Galatians 6:7 - emphasis added
28. Genesis 1:11-12

Chapter 20

1. Mark 4:26-29
2. Galatians 6:7-10 - esp. v9
3. Mark 4:26-27
4. John 12:24
5. 2 Corinthians 9:10 (WE).
6. Matthew 6:1-4
7. Matthew 6:3
8. Matthew 6:4
9. Psalm 18:27
10. Psalm 25:9
11. Proverbs 3:34; James 4:6; 1 Peter 5:5
12. Proverbs 11:2
13. Proverbs 15:33, 18:12
14. Micah 6:8 (NIRV)
15. Micah 6:15 (ERV)
16. Luke 8:15; Galatians 6:7-9
17. 2 Corinthians 5:7

Chapter 21

1. Isaiah 55:10-11 (ERV) - emphasis added
2. Hebrews 4:1-2
3. 1 Corinthians 2:14
4. Proverbs 4:24
5. Joshua 1:1-2
6. Joshua 1:8 - emphasis added
7. Joshua 10:12-14
8. Mark 4:35-41
9. Proverbs 18:21 (AMPC)
10. James 3:3-5
11. Psalm 103:20; Isaiah 55:11
12. Mark 2:11-12; 5:41-42
13. Matthew 8:16
14. Luke 7:14-15; John 11:43-44
15. Joshua 10:12-14; Matthew 8:26; Mark 4:35-41
16. Matthew 21:20-21; Mark 11:23
17. Psalm 141:3 (ERV)
18. Proverbs 18:21
19. Jeremiah 29:11
20. 2 Corinthians 1:20
21. Luke 8:11-15; Romans 10:17
22. Isaiah 55:11 (NIRV)
23. Deuteronomy 28:12; Galatians 6:9

Chapter 22

1. Luke 8:15
2. Proverbs 3:9-10; 11:24-25; 19:17; Luke 6:38; 2 Corinthians 9:10-11
3. Psalm 51:6; John 16:13; 1 John 2:27
4. John 16:12-15
5. James 4:6; 1 Peter 5:5
6. Hosea 4:6
7. Ephesians 2:10

Chapter 23

1. James 1:17
2. Romans 11:29
3. Matthew 5:14-16
4. 1 Corinthians 12:7; 14:12
5. Matthew 5:16; John 15:8

6. Matthew 25:14-30
7. James 1:17
8. 1 Timothy 6:7
9. Jeremiah 29:11
10. Mark 4:18-19; James 5:1-6
11. Colossians 3:1-2
12. 2 Corinthians 4:18
13. Psalm 50:10
14. 1 Corinthians 3:9
15. Lamentations 3:22-23
16. Zechariah 4:10
17. Deuteronomy 8:2; Matthew 6:33
18. Psalm 25:14; Jeremiah 29:11-14; 33:3
19. Psalm 25:12-15; 3 John 2
20. Matthew 16:26; Mark 8:36-37
21. Psalm 37:4

Chapter 24

1. 2 Chronicles 9:1-6; 22-23
2. 2 Chronicles 1:10-12; 9:22-23

Chapter 25

1. Galatians 6:7
2. Isaiah 55:11

Chapter 26

1. Romans 10:17
2. Luke 15:11-32
3. Matthew 6:33
4. Deuteronomy 28:12
5. Romans 13:8
6. Romans 12:2
7. Matthew 14:17-21
8. Matthew 6:33

Chapter 27

1. https://www.moneyandmentalhealth.org/money-and-mental-health-facts/
2. Proverbs 3:9-10
3. Luke 11:13; Galatians 5:22-23

Chapter 28

1. Deuteronomy 28:11-12; 30:5; Proverbs 10:22; 3 John 2
2. Deuteronomy 8:7-10
3. Proverbs 10:15
4. Proverbs 8:17-21
5. Matthew 7:11
6. John 17:3
7. 1 John 4:8, 16
8. Colossians 1:15; Hebrews 1:3
9. John 15:26
10. Romans 5:5
11. Psalm 35:27
12. Psalm 35:27
13. Luke 12:32; 15:11-12 & 31
14. Genesis 1:26
15. Ephesians 4:24
16. John 3:5-8; 1 John 4:15
17. James 1:5
18. John 21:1-3
19. John 21:4-6
20. Matthew 4:18-20
21. John 21:1-14
22. Habakkuk 2:2-3
23. Deuteronomy 28:12 (CEV)

Lightning Source UK Ltd.
Milton Keynes UK
UKHW020635271121
394691UK00006B/299